D1001008

May

To Bob,

Let us work to keep America free & the C.I.A. good.

[signature]

FROM HEALING TO HELL

William Henry Wall, M.D., 1944.

FROM HEALING TO HELL

William Henry Wall, Jr., D.D.S.

NewSouth Books
Montgomery | Louisville

NewSouth Books
P.O. Box 1588
Montgomery, AL 36102

Copyright © 2011 by William Henry Wall, Jr.
All rights reserved under International and Pan-American Copyright
Conventions. Published in the United States by NewSouth Books,
a division of NewSouth, Inc., Montgomery, Alabama.

Library of Congress Cataloging-in-Publication Data

Wall, William Henry, 1937–
From healing to hell / William Henry Wall, Jr.

p. cm.

Includes bibliographical references.

ISBN-13: 978-1-60306-108-7
ISBN-10: 1-60306-108-8

1. Wall, William Henry, 1902-1967. 2. Physicians—Georgia—
Biography. 3. Project MKULTRA. I. Title.
R154.W183W3 2014
610.92—dc22
[B]

2006009847

Composition by Mary Katherine Pappas
Printed in the United States of America
by Sheridan Books

To my mother
for her love, strength, and resolve

And to my father
for his character, integrity, and never-give-up attitude—
a remarkable man with an intense love for his family.

Also, to the victims of the 9/11 terrorist attacks
with the hope the CIA will be returned to an effective agency
for the protection of the citizens of the United States of America.

"When you're going through hell, keep going."

— Winston S. Churchill

Contents

Chapter 1

"Great news, son!"

That night in 1954 when Daddy walked in the door with a big smile on his face, nobody had any idea how relieved I felt. While he was away in the federal prison they called a hospital, smiles at our house had been rare, and since he'd come home we'd barely shared a couple of feeble ones. Tonight's wasn't one of those big beaming smiles from the past, but it was genuine, and in itself that was a blessing.

He waved a couple of red tickets under my nose. "Tomorrow's Labor Day, y'know, and it's the Blakely Lions' last game of the season. Get your work done early, so we can start making up for all the baseball we've missed."

Mother looked up from her desk. "All he has to do is cut the grass."

"I'll get up real early," I said. "It won't take long."

"That's my boy," Daddy said. "And after the game, what d'you say we stop at Charlie's for some oysters on the half shell?"

"You bet!" I actually felt excited again. Watching baseball and eating oysters were the two most fun things Daddy and I used to do together, and memories of those good times still glowed through the gloom of everything that had happened.

It was no use inviting Mother, who didn't care for minor-league baseball or oysters, but she smiled her approval. Daddy laid an arm around my shoulders, and I felt the stored-up tension in my body ease. I grinned as our eyes met, not yet used to being as tall as he.

"It'll be like old times, son," he said. "Guaranteed."

Was such a thing possible? Were we back on solid ground, sharing the happy things we used to share? Had I gotten back the father I'd lost?

I dropped off into a sound sleep that night, hopeful that better days were ahead.

I woke at dawn refreshed, though as I pulled on my shorts I could tell the day would be a good old Georgia scorcher. Pushing our lawn-mower back and forth over the dewy grass gave me plenty of time to reflect. Maybe I could finally stop hanging my head and look people in the eye again.

DADDY ENJOYED the baseball game as much as I did, and as we sat in the stands eating boiled peanuts and commenting on both teams' players, I didn't see a soul whispering behind their hands or even pointing our way. When a great play was made Daddy didn't spring up to yell encouragement the way he used to, but he seemed to enjoy himself.

As for me, I felt reborn.

In a close-run extra inning that brought us all to our feet, the Lions won, and as the stands emptied, Daddy turned cheerful eyes to me. "All right, son, you ready for those oysters?"

"Bet I can eat a peck."

He laughed and walked with me out to our Ford as if nothing out of the ordinary had ever happened. I was glad to walk beside him again proud of the courage he'd shown through his terrible ordeal. Gosh, it felt good to hold my head high after a year and a half of humiliation and loneliness. I welcomed the happy moment for the blessing it was.

Charleston Jones' oyster bar was one of two in town, Daddy's and my favorite hangouts, and both were always crowded after a baseball game. Called Charlie by some, the proprietor was a former Lions pitcher who'd married a local girl and set up in business in Blakely when his ball-playing days ended. Baseball fans and friends liked to come by, eat oysters on the half-shell, and rehash the game.

Daddy had always loved holding forth at Charlie's, laughing and joking with everybody in the place. A big full-of-life man, he never sought center stage, yet center stage was invariably what he got. People loved being in his company. They'd give him the spotlight and come away feeling better for it every time.

We found two empty stools at the counter and ordered our first dozen oysters, my mouth purely watering for those succulent morsels fresh from Apalachicola Bay. Humid Georgia air wafted through the screens that stood in for windows; lazy fans turned overhead. Charlie's wife walked around with a flyswatter, nailing an invader now and again.

While Charlie reached into a big #10 washtub of oysters, wiped his knife on his apron, and began shucking left-handed, I kept an anxious eye on Daddy. Since his release from prison he'd often seemed subdued and distracted, but when I saw him looking around with the familiar twinkle in his eye, I rested easy. He nodded and smiled to the other patrons like his old jovial self.

A local character called Pete reached out a bony paw. "I tell you what, Doc, it sure is great to have you back!"

Daddy's face lit up. "Pete, you old scoundrel. Mighty glad to be back, too."

Pete looked me over. "This no-count scarecrow ain't Little Doc, is it?"

"Yes sirree," Daddy said. "Gonna make a sure-enough doctor out of him, so he can take over and let me retire."

"Now, Doc, don't you talk about retiring." Pete shook his head. "We need you 'round here. I already like to died while you was gone."

"Is that so?" Daddy's face showed real concern.

"I wouldn't lie to you. Took the pneumonia, and ain't nobody like you for the pneumonia. I told the old lady, if Doc Wall was here I'd of got well overnight."

Daddy laughed and slapped him on the back. "Come on, you can lay off the soft soap now you're on your feet again."

I was hungrily watching Charlie. He had over a dozen glistening oysters shucked and arranged on Bakelite trays that had jostled so many shells they'd lost all their shine.

Pete said, "Yep, I'm doing right fair now. But like I told you, when we needed us a good doctor, you was gone, and that hurt me awful bad."

Daddy was lining up bottles of hot sauce in readiness for the oysters. "Well, Pete, in a few more years your worries will be over. When this boy finishes medical school you'll have you a fine doctor for sure."

Pete jabbed a gentle punch at my arm. "All right, boy, get on with it!"

I grinned half-heartedly. In the wake of our troubles my high school grades had sunk so low I had few hopes of getting into medical school. If I couldn't, it would crush Daddy, so I kept my doubts to myself. He'd already had enough disappointment to last a lifetime.

Charlie set two trays of oysters on the counter in front of us, and Daddy helped himself to saltines, ready to consume with gusto.

"Y'all take it easy," Pete said as we settled down to enjoy our briny feast. "See you around."

"You bet." Daddy tucked a paper napkin over his tie. "Now then, son, let's see who can eat the hottest oyster tonight."

By the time we were done, we'd put away four dozen apiece. Daddy was home, the good old days were back.

FOR THE FIRST SIXTEEN YEARS OF MY LIFE, wherever Doctor W. H. Wall went, I was likely to be right by his side. His shadow—Little Doc. That's what folks called me, and I loved both the name and the association. Hundreds of times he carried me along when he drove out in the country to make house calls. Every family greeted him like a savior.

Sometimes I followed him inside to wait in the front room, sometimes I hung around the porch or the yard talking to the kids if they weren't too shy, maybe playing with the family dog or just wait in the car listening to WWL and Bugling Sam Decomel in New Orleans. I had to limit the use of the car radio for fear I would kill the battery. Daddy was very attentive to the condition of his car and always kept it in perfect working order.

After he'd done his best for the patient and we got back in our car to leave, whomever waved goodbye always beamed gratitude and relief. But the most memorable times were when we'd pull up outside a crossroads store. "Come on, son," Daddy would say. "Let's go politick a little and chew the fat." Anybody in the neighborhood who saw his car heading for the store would drop what they were doing to hustle down there too.

No more than five years old when I first tagged along, I was puzzled about that fat, for I never saw anybody chew any. Soon I learned it was just a saying. To Daddy, chew the fat meant listen to whatever the other fellows wanted to say, then tell them what he thought.

As soon as we walked into the store he'd say, "All right, son, have you some crackers and vienna sausage," or sometimes "Have you some crackers and hoop cheese." Then he'd ask, "What kind of bellywash you want?"—his name for soda pop. I'd take an R. C. Cola, sometimes a Coke.

So he'd set me up with my snack, then do what he'd promised—chew the fat with the storekeeper and politick with the folks crowding in to unload their troubles, swap jokes, or just shake his hand. Watching him in that setting was watching a people person to the nth degree. The folks of Early County knew it and responded in kind.

One stunt he loved to perform always mystified his onlookers. "All right, now," he'd say, "I'm taking bets." He would go behind the counter, lean both arms on it, and scan the spectators' faces.

Then, with all the gravity of a conjuror: "Watch carefully, now, because I'm fixin to cut a one-pound piece off this wheel of cheese. Not *almost* one pound, not a little *over* a pound. *Exactly* one pound. Any bets I can't do it?"

Somebody would always wager a nickel or a dime—in the rural South these were poverty days. Daddy would flex his wrists, shoot his cuffs, take up the cutter, and reduce that wheel of cheese by precisely one pound—not half an ounce more, not half an ounce less.

The onlookers always shook their heads. "Ain't that the derndest thing? Doc, how in tarnation you do that? You ain't missed it by a hair!"

Daddy would just laugh and tell them to keep their money. As a youngster back in the family store at Wall's Crossing he'd done the identical thing a hundred times, and he knew he'd never fail.

The way those folks treated him, you'd have thought the President had stopped by. Wide-eyed children gaped as if he were Santy Claus. Bursting with pride, I ate my country-store picnic and basked in their admiration for Daddy, adding my own for the easy way he joked and smiled, the way he listened and dealt patiently with their various woes. He had a good word for every person there, because he truly cared about each one—that was plain to see. And in my own young eyes, Daddy was the next thing to God.

Those were magical times, being Little Doc, heir apparent to Blakely's beloved Doctor Wall, before the bubble burst and the troubles came. Afterward, those long months while Daddy was in prison left a hole in my soul, and the only thing that kept me going was praying that hole could get patched up and life could get back to normal. Just sixteen years old when they sent him away, I clung to that desperate hope with all the strength of a mature man.

HOME FROM THE OYSTER BAR in the sweltering summer night, I had been asleep for a couple of hours, my bedroom dark as a cave, when heavy hands woke me up, ripping at my pajama pants.

"Hey, cut it out!" I hollered. "What's going on?" I bolted upright, trying to hang onto my pants.

Daddy's voice shook the walls. "You goddamn little mother-fucker— I'll show you! I'll give you what you deserve!" He went on jerking at my pajamas.

I couldn't believe what was happening, what I heard. Daddy never cursed or used such words—never.

"Whoa, Daddy!" I yelled. "Hold off!"

I kicked out to defend myself, while he went on cursing and tearing at my pants, pummeling me like a wild man. Still in the dark, we hollered and thrashed around as I struggled to beat him off. I scrambled to my knees, then got on my feet, desperate to get the bed between us. Nothing made sense.

He roared on. "Goddamn you, you little bastard! You mother-fucking son of a bitch!"

"Wait, Daddy! Wait! Hold on! What's this about?"

He just kept shouting and throwing wild punches. "Don't think you can fool me! I know the filthy things you and your mother got up to while I was gone! That S.O.B. Isbell was right, you damn mother-fucker!"

"My God, Daddy, what're you talking about?"

"You can't hide it from me—I know all about it! Every night, going at it, you and her. I'll fix you! I'll fix you both!"

I hopped around dodging his blows, unable to believe the fury, the accusations, or the language spewing from his lips. A raging gorilla bursting into my room couldn't have shocked me more. Suddenly I was no longer a six-foot teenager but a terrified kid.

"Please, Daddy, listen! You've got everything all wrong!"

When I managed to switch on the bedside lamp I saw that although it was the middle of the night, he was still completely clothed. His distorted face confirmed what I already knew: my father was out of his mind.

"Mother!" I yelled. "Come quick, help me! Daddy's gone crazy!"

"Crazy, huh?" He snatched up my baseball bat from the corner and lunged at me. "You little mother-fucker, I'll show you who's crazy! I'll beat you to death!"

I had picked up the desk chair to hold him off when Mother, barefoot and in her nightgown, came running into my room.

"Henry, for God's sake!" She dragged at Daddy's suit coat with both hands. "What's come over you? Stop it! The boy hasn't done a thing!"

I scrambled on the floor for the jeans I'd tossed there at bedtime, while Daddy shook Mother off and went on swinging wildly, cursing and screaming.

"Don't think you can fool me! I know what nasty doings you were up to while I was gone! Animals, low-lifes! A filthy little bastard, that's what he is!"

"My God, Henry, please!" Mother pulled at his arm, struggling to draw him toward the door.

I simply could not believe what was happening. I had never known Daddy to use a foul word, never known him to lay a hand on me. How could he do all this and concoct such an evil fantasy of lies?

Mother's efforts seemed futile. She was crying, but she wouldn't stop pleading nor pulling at him. "Henry, you have to stop this! Leave him alone!"

When he drew back a fist to swing at her, I shouted, "Let him be,

Mother! Just turn loose and run, go call for help. I'll knock him down."

But she wouldn't abandon me to fight him on my own—she renewed her efforts to pull him away. I considered trying to get the bat away from him to use it myself, but that maniacal look on his face warned me off. All I could do was shelter behind my chair while Daddy thrashed and swore. When a hysterical urge to laugh rose up inside me, I knew letting it out might cost me my life.

At last Mother got a better purchase on his arm. She spoke soothingly, urging him toward the hall.

"Henry, come on now. Listen, there's a phone call, one of your patients is in labor. You have to calm down! They need you."

Of course the phone hadn't rung. But her ruse seemed to work. The physician in Daddy was still alive, and he'd always put his patients' needs first. His arms dropped, then his shoulders, as the fury leached out of his face.

Mother went on encouraging, placating. "That's right, Henry. That's right. Come on, now." Her intuition—or inspiration—had short-circuited his mad rampage. "Hurry, now, this man who called, he says they need you right away."

I didn't know what she would tell him when they got to the phone, but seeing her handle this part, I figured she could manage that as well. The worst had passed.

After she coaxed him into the hall I stood there in a daze, half-naked, unable to make sense of a thing—our happy time together at the ball game, good oysters and fun at Charlie's place, falling asleep lulled by fresh hope, only to be catapulted into a life-or-death struggle with an insane stranger.

I was devastated. My idol had turned on me, accused me of unspeakable things, called me the filthiest of names. It was as if some demon had spouted foul words through my dearly loved daddy's lips. If anyone else had said those things to me, I'd have beaten him senseless. But this was my adored father.

Dear Lord in Heaven, what had happened to Doctor Wall and Little

Doc? What could I do? Again, I wanted to run away, go tearing out into the night and just keep running, running, running till I collapsed. But how could I leave Mother to cope with such a mess? There was no way out, none at all.

I walked over and closed the door to the hall, sank down on the side of my bed, and gave way to shaking sobs. It was the bleakest hour of my life.

So great were the horror and pain of that night that for fifty years I couldn't tell a soul about it. I didn't even tell Mother of his worst accusation, the vilest name he had hurled at me. I just told her he'd burst into my room suddenly in the dark and attacked me for no reason at all.

Thirty minutes later Daddy's voice reached me from the kitchen. "Son, can you come in here for a minute?" More bewilderment, because he sounded perfectly normal again.

Weak-kneed, I ventured out to find him and Mother sitting at the kitchen table. The storm had obviously passed. As he sat there waiting for me, I saw him as a sick, worried old man. And Daddy was only fifty-two.

"Son," he said, "I want you and your mother to know how terribly, terribly sorry I am. I wouldn't have had this happen for all the world. I don't know what came over me to make me do such a thing."

Still shaken, Mother and I listened in silence.

"You know, I told you back in January they were giving me something up there in Lexington to make me lose my mind. Nothing else could make me act as crazy as I have tonight. For the life of me, I just don't know what it was." The remorse and sadness on his face tore at my heart.

Mother and I exchanged glances—me still sniffling from recent tears, her eyes red and her hands clenched.

She shook her head. "Henry, Henry," was all she said. I didn't say a word, for I didn't know what to say. It was over, that was the main thing. But would it happen again?

FROM THAT HOUR ON, Mother, Daddy, and I all recognized that something was terribly wrong with him, and we had no idea what it was. He'd left for prison diabetic and overweight, yet drug-free and thoroughly sane. He came back to us minus seventy pounds but seemingly all right otherwise—until that hideous 2:00 a.m. when his demons came out to play.

Daddy never mentioned the episode again, nor did Mother and I talk about it any more. We were too afraid and too ashamed. I'd never seen a human being in such a violent rage, much less my self-possessed, respectable Daddy. That hellish attack without a second's warning knocked all the props from under me, plunging me into confusion and back to deep despair. What a fool I'd been, daring to hope. Nothing would ever come right again.

Not many days passed before I discovered some dark stains where my underpants covered my skin. When I mentioned it to Mother, she said she'd found the same thing in hers. By cautious questioning, we discovered to our hurt and horror that Daddy—still paranoid, still obsessed with his incest fantasy—had put silver nitrate in our underwear. He believed this ruse would prove the truth of his accusations. After that we knew our nightmare might never end.

The maniacal look I first saw on Daddy's face that night was to appear again and again, always without warning, inevitably with the direst consequences. We were caught up in a Greek tragedy with no way out. Over the coming years Daddy and I were fated to re-enact our mortal struggle in many settings and forms. Whatever dreadful thing had befallen him in that prison hospital would haunt my parents as long as they lived. And for half a century it would also haunt me, his only son.

Struggle was something Daddy knew a great deal about, and I was brought up on his story. As much a legend of my childhood as Tom Mix or the Hardy Boys, its details were as familiar as if Daddy's story were my own. His family was well established at Wall's Crossing in Schley County, four miles outside Ellaville—successful business-people and farmers dating back a hundred years. There the name of Wall was revered, and as Daddy's best friend Dr. McCall "Mac" Calhoun put it, "In Schley County the Walls are like leaves on the trees." Faith, family, honesty, and hard work were the basics young Henry Wall grew up with, and in the light of his clan's reputation he could have set up in practice at home and done well.

But the easy route was never to be his fate. Although from a young age he wanted to become a doctor, his education did not fall in his lap. He worked hard for it, starting in the one-room Glen Holley School, progressing to a technical school, then to Gordon Institute where he excelled in sports and marksmanship, and eventually graduating from the University of Georgia in 1922. After his acceptance to the Medical College of Georgia, his pleased father continued helping him financially along the way.

At MCG the work was hard, and Henry strove to do well. Naïvely, he made an early mistake, buying his microscope at a bargain price from a fellow who had flunked out rather than paying full price for a new one. Janie Turner, the dean's spinster secretary and jealous guardian of the microscope concession, kept Henry Wall in her sights from that day on.

By springtime the first-year students heard of a fearsome practice called "nut-cutting" that marked the end of each MCG year. The bottom twenty percent of the class was flunked out, and Janie Turner singled out the flunkees. Already in her bad books, Henry proceeded thereafter with extreme care.

His prospects soon became more ominous. When results of the pathology exam were posted, though Henry had correctly identified most specimens (including a cyst excised from his own back), Janie Turner had marked a failing grade beside his name. Rather than risk being flunked out at nut-cutting time, in May he quietly dropped out of school and set out in search of a job.

Months passed before Wall's Crossing got the bad news. Chagrined and unaccustomed to failure, Henry postponed telling his family until his father asked pointed questions about his progress. At that Henry confessed he had left medical school to work for the Monroe Calculator Company—a job he performed well and would hold for several years.

For part of that time he lived in western North Carolina, taking advantage of the region's land boom to sell real estate in addition to his other job. He was carrying on a long-distance courtship by then with Miss Hallie Walker, a former schoolmate and music teacher from Americus, Georgia, and when Atlanta's new radio station WSB invited her to perform, he sent her a telegram from Hendersonville complimenting the "Pianist Extraordinaire."

Yet his determination to succeed in medicine still burned. Five years after his first start, Henry entered the University of Alabama's two-year medical program in Tuscaloosa. The prospect of slogging through those same first-year subjects again didn't deter him, or the eventual necessity to complete his degree at some other, four-year school. He simply forged ahead, prepared to cross each bridge as he reached it.

Again his father helped to underwrite the cost of his studies. At the university, Henry completed those first-year subjects and was well into his second year when one November day in 1928 brought a telegram from his brother: HURRY HOME DADDY DYING.

Luckily, Henry had a rail pass, because his family sold train tickets at their Wall's Crossing store. Without hesitating, he dropped everything to rush to the depot and board the first southbound passenger train. He had barely found a seat before he heard a familiar voice.

"Mist' Henry, what you doing on this train? Going down to Florida to have you some fun?"

He looked up at the smiling porter's face and recognized a man who had grown up near Ellaville. "Well, well—Sylvester Proctor. How've you been?"

"Doing fine, Mist' Henry. How's all your folks?"

"Mighty sad right now. I just had a telegram from my brother saying our daddy's at death's door." He glanced out the window to check on the train's progress. "I just pray I make it home in time."

"I sure am sorry to hear that. I hope you'll s'cuse me, Mist' Henry, making that joke 'bout Florida, I didn't know." Suddenly the porter frowned. "But hold on a minute. This here's the Seminole Limited—it don't never stop at Wall's Crossing."

"I know," Henry said. Day after day during his boyhood, when the slower trains stopped to take on water near the family store, he'd climbed aboard to sell the passengers drinks, cigarettes, and snacks. And just as often he'd stood watching as the crack express trains flew by.

"Mist' Henry, how you going to get home?"

"Get off at the first stop, hitch a ride back."

"No, sir, that ain't no good. You needing to get home right quick, and you be too far down the road. I'll just walk on up through the train here, speak to the engineer. If I tell him it's you and you got death in the family, I expect he'll stop at Wall's crossing to let you off."

Henry's eyes filled up. "If you can do that for me, Sylvester—"

"You just leave it to me." The porter was already on his way.

The miles clicked by, fields and pine trees, woods and swamps, while Henry hoped and prayed. Sure enough, within a few miles of Wall's Crossing he felt the train's forward movement slow. He made his way quickly to the vestibule where Sylvester waited and pressed a folded bill into the porter's hand.

"I won't forget this, Sylvester. If ever I can do anything for you, you let me know."

"Don't be worrying 'bout me, Mist' Henry. You just get on home."

The moment Sylvester let down the steps, Henry was off the train. But his heart sank before the train even pulled out, for in the front yard of his family's large frame house stood a collection of cars, trucks, buggies, and wagons. He was too late to do anything but mourn. Dead of a ruptured gall bladder, his father lay in his casket in the front room.

With a sad heart Henry returned to Alabama and completed that second year. With two more to go, his spirits lifted when the University of Pennsylvania accepted him. Yet by midsummer more disappointment was to come, for his father's death had left family finances too tight to cover the costs. Back to work he went.

In October, when the stock market crashed, banks closed, and men jumped out of windows on Wall Street, he viewed the national calamity as one more hurdle to overcome. His sweetheart Hallie wrote him that ten prominent men in Americus had committed suicide within a week. When other young men might have given up, Henry kept working toward his goal.

He put his pride in his back pocket and wrote a letter asking for an appointment with Dr. G. Lombard Kelley, then in charge of admissions at MCG. When that letter went unanswered he wrote another, and still with no response, followed up with telephone calls. He was never put through to Dr. Kelley, and Dr. Kelley never returned a single call. No man to be deterred, Henry had already learned that Janie Turner no longer held nut-cutting powers, so he traveled to Augusta to clear the way for a new start.

He presented himself at Dr. Kelley's office, where Janie Turner told him to have a seat and wait. He waited for hours. Finally Dr. Kelley happened to walk out into the waiting room and saw him there.

"Why, Henry Wall," he said. "What are you doing here?"

"Waiting to see you," Henry said. "I've been waiting most of the day."

Dr. Kelley reached out to shake his hand. "I'm glad to see you, mighty sorry you had to wait. Step in the office here. How many years has it been? Three or four?" He indicated a chair across from his own.

Henry sat down. "No sir, it's been seven years since I matriculated here."

"Seven! Goodness, time gets away. Frankly, I was surprised when you dropped out—I believed you had the makings of a fine physician. I wish you had come and discussed your difficulties with me."

"Yes sir, I wish I had too. Anyway, I'd like to try again."

"Good for you. What have you been doing in the meantime?"

Henry flashed his big trademark smile. "Worked for a business-machines company for four years, then completed two years of medicine at the University of Alabama. After I decided to try again I hoped you would answer my letters."

"What letters?"

"Why, Doctor Kelley, I've written you several times, asking for an appointment."

Dr. Kelley cocked his head, a frown furrowing his brow. "Henry, I never received your letters."

"Well, I wrote, repeatedly, and after that I phoned."

"I've never heard a word of this," Dr. Kelley said. "I must certainly look into it."

Henry understood then what had happened. Janie Turner had blocked his efforts, discarded his letters, never passed on word that he'd phoned.

Dr. Kelley said, "Did you see Mr. Derrick in the waiting room?"

"Not if you mean the Derrick that flunked out of my class."

"That's the one. Janie said he was waiting to see me."

"I've been waiting most of the day, and Derrick hasn't been here. Maybe she got the two of us confused."

"Well, congratulations on your perseverance, though I'm really not surprised."

Henry said, "Here's my transcript from Alabama," and handed it over.

Minutes crept by while Dr. Kelley studied it, then sat back and folded his hands. "I see you've done well. We'll be happy to have you here again."

Henry relaxed and let out the breath he had been holding. At last something was working out in his favor. "I'm mighty grateful, Doctor Kelley."

"You're a deserving young man. But there is just one problem. We can't accept these credits from Alabama."

Henry could hardly believe what he'd heard. "Can't accept them? You mean I'll have to start over?"

"I'm afraid so. The year you did here was incomplete, and the Alabama credits don't transfer." Doctor Kelley studied him intently. "Is starting over more than you're willing to face?"

"No sir," said the eternal optimist. "I'll do whatever it takes."

So Henry enrolled in those same first-year subjects for the *third* time. His subsequent progress was outstanding, and as he moved along through the second and third years, his interest in Miss Hallie Walker rose to fever pitch. They had already courted for seven years, but the difficulty was that no married student could graduate from MCG. His matrimonial resolve was as strong as his resolve to become a physician, however, and in September of his senior year they were secretly wed.

He had begun that school year with a total capital of fifty dollars and soon had to go to the dean to say he was running out of money and couldn't last much longer. This time luck was with him, for the dean put him in touch with a philanthropist, William D. Chapple, trustee, M. L. Williams trust that liked to assist medical students in financial distress. Henry wrote his letter, and when the man wrote back wanting to know how much he needed to finish school, Henry answered that he needed $150 right away, another $150 at the start of the new year. He expressed his gratitude and promised to repay the loan just as soon as he was in practice and could earn enough to do so. The Salem, MA student fund saved him.

The first check arrived promptly, and in January the second one, along with a note saying there was no need to repay the money, as it came from a special trust established for that very purpose. Never one to forget a kindness, every year thereafter as long as his benefactor lived Henry sent him a shipment of Georgia peaches and pecans.

By graduation time it had taken Henry seven years to earn his degree, while making an academic record that surpassed most of his peers'. He was named to the Sydenstricker Seminar for clinical excellence, and on graduation day the young Mrs. Wall must have been thrilled to see her husband awarded the M.D. degree with honor at last.

After the couple announced their marriage, he moved his bride to Plains, Georgia, where he would serve a brief internship at the Wise Clinic. (One of the nurses working there at the time would later become world-famous as "Miss Lillian" Carter, mother of a U.S. President.) Henry then moved to join an older physician in the tiny Wilcox County community of Pitts, and Hallie taught school until they learned a child was on the way. In May of 1934 when her time came to be delivered, they traveled back to Plains so that Hallie Anne Wall could be born at Wise Clinic.

Henry ran for the office of mayor of Pitts and tied his opponent for the job with each candidate getting fewer than ten votes. Before a runoff election could be held he happened to meet a traveler named Claude Howell, who spoke of a crying need in his own South Georgia town.

"Doctor Wall, why don't you relocate? I own a drugstore in Blakely, and if you'll come, my pharmacist Robert Hall and I will do everything we can to help you build your practice. There's a small office space in the rear of the drugstore where you can set up, as soon as you like. It's a good-sized town, twenty thousand in the county, and you have no idea how badly we need a well-trained, up-to-date doctor like yourself."

Henry made a visit to Blakely and saw the need for himself. After talking it over with Hallie, he decided to make the move. So on July 4, 1935, he and Hallie and baby Anne came to Blakely to live. Though the times were beyond uncertain, Henry set up a little office in back of Howell Drug Company, moving a short time later to a second-floor space across North Main on the north side of the courthouse square.

It was an act of courage and optimism, setting out to establish a medical practice in a hard-hit agricultural community. He surely didn't move expecting to get rich, for the whole country was in the throes of the Great Depression. His motive was the one that governed his whole life: serving human need. Two years later I would arrive to complete the family.

South Georgia was, and still is, farming country, and in the 1930s many farm families all but starved. Business was at a standstill, the boll weevil had done its worst, hard times prevailed. Walker Evans and James Agee graphically recorded the era's poverty and hopelessness in their classic *Let Us Now Praise Famous Men*—gaunt men and barefoot women, malnourished children in filthy rags, tenant shacks so dilapidated they hardly gave shelter from the rain.

While the town had several other physicians, there was no shortage of sick folks. Tuberculosis, malaria, rickets, injuries from farm work—as the patients began to come he saw them all, including many with other maladies common in that pre-antibiotic age. He never dreamed his advent might provoke envy among his competitors, because he'd come to Blakely to serve.

Soon after he arrived he began to build his reputation as a good "pneumonia doctor" during a fearsome epidemic of influenza and pneumonia. Because he knew about the success of sulfa drugs he was able to save many lives, while other doctors' patients often died. Daily he met many challenges. Malnutrition was widespread, particularly the nutritional deficiency known as pellagra. Although Blakely was peanut country, people found it strange that Daddy recommended eating lots of peanuts raw—he knew they supplied niacin, a vitamin that the diet of pellagra sufferers lacked.

His battle against malaria became personal a few years later, when my five-year-old sister Anne came down with the disease. A neighboring family invited her on a picnic to a rural swimming place and brought her home covered in insect bites. Daddy gave Mother the dickens for letting Anne go, and when she came down with chills and fever, he knew it had to be malaria and treated her appropriately.

Patients quickly responded to Daddy's skills and unfailing respect, and his earthy wit lightened many a sickroom. Working twelve to fourteen-hour days almost from the start, he delivered babies, cured pneumonia, took out tonsils, and set fractures that healed straight—the latter something of a rarity in Blakely, as he soon found out. Before Daddy came to town, many townspeople with broken limbs wound up with crooked arms and curiously warped legs. After one doctor put a cast on incorrectly, a prominent man in town had to have his gangrenous leg amputated. Daddy, on the other hand, got excellent results. He kept up with the latest developments in medicine, and Blakely's first x-ray machine was the one installed in his office.

During his first years there, he charged one dollar for office visits and three dollars for a house call, though hard times meant he frequently went unpaid. He often seemed embarrassed even to ask for those low fees, for he knew how tough things were for most people in the county. A day's income might be four dollars, or it might be nothing at all. Most obstetrical deliveries still took place in the mother's home, the handful of better-off families as well as the poor. His fee for delivering a baby was twenty-five dollars. Not all local doctors delivered the babies of the poor. Daddy did and rarely was paid.

Although he was by no means making a fortune, he was soon earning both a decent living and a fine professional reputation. My friend Bob Hall, son of Robert Hall, Sr., who runs a thriving drugstore on the courthouse square today, told me, "Your dad deserves a lot more credit than he's been given, because he brought modern medicine to Early County." I've heard Daddy's friend Dr. Mac Calhoun say the same. Patients knew it and responded, but the town's other physicians didn't like it, and jealousies grew.

An idealist, at first Daddy had no idea of forces at work behind the scenes, and it took him some time to discover that Blakely's power lay in the hands of a few men, often unscrupulous.

Chapter 2

It's the perfect small-town, Deep South movie set. Blakely, Georgia, has its central square with a picturesque county courthouse, thriving churches, a modern hospital, small businesses, and surrounding farms. It has families who've been there for decades, and it has its characters, idols, and ideals. The giant chain and discount stores haven't even invaded this quiet town.

Hundreds of good people live in Blakely, both white and black. Asians have come to Early County to operate a restaurant and manage the motels. Brown-and-white signs marked "To Historic District" indicate the old route into town, while the Highway 27 bypass stretches through vast fields planted to peanuts and cotton, watered by great wheeled arcs that roll over the flat ground. Northward, a quiet country road leads to the evocative silence of the Kolomoki Mounds, an ancient ceremonial center created by Swift Creek and Weeden Island Indians over a thousand years ago. A few miles to the west flows the murky Chattahoochee River, well on its way to the Gulf of Mexico.

Back in town beside the railroad tracks ranks of red-peanut-hauling trailers wait in readiness for this year's crop. Along Blakely's shady streets white-columned porches mark pretty, modest houses, while on the outskirts a few more pretentious places can be seen. Azaleas and wisteria dress the springtime scene.

Most Blakely children grow up in families who tell them how lucky they are to live in such a nice place. A few restless or super-ambitious teenagers fret to venture out into the big world, though half a lifetime later they'll yearn to retire to just such a spot. Nowadays in the soft evenings young people bring their cars and trucks to the somnolent courthouse square and congregate around the headlights with their music and their light-hearted laughter. On the surface, Blakely is a very peaceful place.

It wasn't always so. When Daddy came to Blakely to live, racism was rampant in South Georgia and violence against blacks common—encouraged by "The Wild Man from Sugar Creek," Governor Eugene Talmadge, and his minions. A county-seat bully by the name of Sid Howell, known to local blacks as "the high sheriff," was one of those minions, and even before I started school I'd heard Sheriff Howell was a man to fear. Known to make all arrests at gunpoint, he kept the colored people terrified and the whites wary. A young friend of mine with good reason to know claimed that, in the course of making arrests, Sheriff Howell had killed more than twenty men, most of them colored.

I was only a toddler, too young to remember it, but Anne well remembers a night when Daddy drove Mother and us children in his 1939 Ford coupé down to the northeast corner of the courthouse square, in front of the old wooden jail. In small towns in those days before television, any out-of-the-ordinary event brought out the curious, which must explain why he took us to see such a ghastly sight.

Clearly visible through the jail's open front door was the lifeless body of a colored man, dangling from the rope that had hanged him. He had been executed on the spot—lynched—with the door left open to give all who passed a view of the grisly scene.

My sister was left with a lifelong belief that our county jail was a horrible place and our sheriff and his jailer loathsome—a belief I would soon come to share. Although the old jail was later replaced by a new brick building across from the livery stable and mule barn on River Street, the sheriff's violent reputation never changed.

As for Daddy, his attitude toward blacks was the polar opposite of Sid Howell's. True, he had grown up in Georgia, but he treated every person and every family with dignity and respect regardless of whether they were rich or poor, white or black. Blacks accounted for nearly three-quarters of Early County's population, so they made up most of Daddy's patient load. He must have made thousands of house calls all over our large county, and on the many occasions when he took me with him, I saw his even-handed treatment for myself. He truly loved his patients and loved helping them, whoever they were.

During the 1930s and early 1940s Georgia's rabidly segregationist Governor Gene Talmadge was hell-bent on keeping black people down, encouraging terror tactics to deny them their vote and all other civil rights. That kind of thing was an anathema to Daddy, but unfortunately, Ol' Gene's race-baiting won him wide support among hidebound white farmers and others with racist views. And in every sense Sheriff Sid Howell was a Talmadge man.

Daddy's first significant encounter with him happened when Sheriff Howell came over to his office to enlist Daddy's help in committing a deranged black woman to the insane asylum. The other member of the team was the local ordinary, a justice by the name of D. C. Morgan, known to one and all as Babe.

"I'll help if I can," Daddy told him, "but I'll have to examine her first."

"Ne'mind that," the sheriff said. "All you have to do is sign, and she goes."

Daddy leaned back in his desk chair. "Now, Sheriff, let's suppose for a minute that somebody was wanting to commit you."

The sheriff bristled, but Daddy went on. "If that were the case, would you want me to send you to the asylum without seeing you?"

Sheriff Howell shifted uneasily in his seat. "Well . . . I reckon when you put it like that . . ."

Reluctantly he drove Daddy and Morgan out to the family's house, supplying background on the way. "This little farm here belonged to Annie's and Dumah's parents—not sharecropping, they owned it outright. It's Dumah's now. After their mama died, this Annie kept house for Dumah . . . till she went crazy, that is."

He propped an elbow on the sill of his open window and shot his passengers a sidewise glance. "'Y'all know making moonshine's illegal, but if you want some of the best"—he chuckled—"Dumah's the nigger to see."

Daddy managed to keep his mouth shut, but it wasn't easy.

In spite of the hard times, as the car drew up in front of the place Daddy saw no sign of want. A garden flourished at one side of the house, along with a penful of chickens and a fattening hog. The unpainted house and outbuildings were neat and clean, as was the freshly swept yard.

"Moonshining must pay right well," Morgan said.

"You damn right," the sheriff said. "See there on the front porch, that's the nigger bootlegger I was telling you about."

A nervous-looking colored man came down the steps to meet them. "Y'all gentlemens come on in. Sister Annie, she setting right there in the front room. You ain't got to talk to her no more'n a few minutes 'fore you see her mind done gone. It's got so I can't leave the house and her in it, scared she'll set it afire."

Smoke curled upward from the drooping cigarette in a corner of the sheriff's mouth. "Liable to keep you away from your business down in the woods, won't it?"

Dumah nodded, serious. "Yes, sir, it sure do keep me away from my business—you know I raises cotton and corn."

"That's all, huh? Well, come on," the sheriff said. "Let's get it over with."

When Dumah held the door open for them, Morgan said, "Doctor Wall, you'll have the final word, so why don't you go in first?"

Daddy took off his hat, went in, and sat down in a chair beside the woman. "Hello, Annie, I'm Doctor Wall. How're you feeling today?"

The other three followed Daddy to watch. Annie sat with a tattered Bible in her lap, staring straight ahead and picking at a sore on her leg.

Daddy indicated his fellow visitors. "This is Sheriff Howell, and this is Mister Morgan, a friend of ours from town. Your brother's worried about you, and he asked us to come out and see you."

She scowled, folding her arms. "All y'all devils get outta here. I ain't studying none of you."

Her brother laid a hand on her shoulder. "Girl, you better behave yourself. The doctor come to see you because you know you ain't been doing too good."

Daddy was reaching for her wrist to feel her pulse and note the texture of her skin when she shook him loose. "You get your hands off of me. I ain't studying nobody."

Daddy leaned back then, as if he had all day to sit and chat. "Tell me, Annie, has Dumah been giving you plenty to eat? You have a pretty good appetite?"

Dumah answered for her. "Yes sir, she sure can eat. Sunup to sundown, but she don't eat one thing but cornbread. I ain't never seen nobody so crazy about cornbread."

"How about her bowels?"

"Well, sir, they working overtime. Annie run out back twenty times a day."

"Has she had those sores long?"

Dumah said, "Annie, how long you had them sores?"

Annie opened her Bible and pretended to read.

Sid Howell threw his still-burning cigarette to the floor and stepped on it, then poked another, unlit, in the corner of his mouth. "Seen enough, Doc? You ready to sign?"

Daddy ignored him. "Dumah, I tell you what let's do. Let's change her diet. Don't give her any more cornbread—not even a bite. And I want you to see that she eats *lots* of raw peanuts."

Dumah shook his head. "She going to raise the devil. We got a plenty of peanuts, but Annie want her cornbread."

"Let her raise the devil, then, but just do as I say. Get rid of your meal so she can't have any cornbread, and give her plenty of raw peanuts. I don't think she's been getting enough vitamins, and peanuts are loaded with a vitamin she needs."

"All right, then, Doctor, I'll do like you say."

Daddy turned to Annie, who by now was watching him out of the corner of her eye. "Now, Annie, we want you to get better, and I believe you will if you'll quit eating cornbread and just eat what Dumah gives you. Can you promise me you won't eat any more cornbread?"

Still no answer, but Daddy could tell she heard.

Sheriff Howell got out his matches and moved for the door. "You aren't going to sign the papers, are you?"

"Not yet," Daddy said.

"Huh. Then I reckon we came way out here for nothing."

"Maybe not." Daddy stood up and patted Annie on the shoulder. "A month from now, Annie, I want Dumah to bring you in town to see me. I expect you'll feel a lot better by then."

Suddenly Annie jumped up and commenced to flap her skirt at an empty corner of the room. "Who let them chickens in here?"

"Hush, girl," Dumah said. "You talking fool talk. Ain't no chickens there. You gentlemens see, that's the way she been carrying on."

"Let's us four step out on the porch," Daddy said. Howell, Morgan, and Dumah followed, while Annie went on making shooing motions with her skirt.

Daddy said, "I don't believe there's anything serious wrong with her mind. I'm ninety-nine percent sure she's suffering from pellagra. Not enough variety in her diet, too few vitamins. It all fits the picture—her mind being affected, the loose bowels, those sores on her skin.

"So let's just see how she gets along. She'll get plenty of niacin from the peanuts, which I believe she needs. Then if she's no better we'll talk about sending her away."

Dumah still looked dubious. "You telling me peanuts can clear Annie mind?"

Daddy nodded. "I expect after a month you'll see quite a change. By then you can go on about your business, not worry about her one bit."

On the drive back to town Sid Howell grumbled. "No sense taking up so damn much time with a crazy nigger. She belongs in the asylum and you two know it. If we don't put her away, next thing she'll haul off and kill somebody, or set the house afire."

From the back seat Morgan laughed. "Come on, Sheriff, you're not worried about Annie. I reckon your liquor supply down at the jail's run low, and you want to get Dumah back to making whiskey so you can arrest him and confiscate his stock."

Sid Howell turned cold eyes toward the back seat. "You accusing me of something?"

"Just a joke, Sheriff. Anyhow, Doc's got a point. With so many folks going hungry, pellagra may well be what she's got. She won't be the first, I know that."

After they dropped Daddy at his office and he had time to think it over, it dawned on him that the sheriff was furious, made to stand aside while Daddy took control. He'd lost face in front of Morgan, which was a big deal. And he'd also lost face in front of a deranged woman and her bootlegger brother—both blacks—which for Sid Howell was a *very* big deal.

A month later to the day, Dumah came in to Daddy's office bringing Annie, bright as a button and clearly in robust health. "Doctor, you sure told us right. Annie ain't et no cornbread in four weeks, and not a thing in God's world wrong with her mind no more. I can go on out the house any time, do what I have to do. Annie, ain't that so?"

She ducked her head and held up a hand to hide her grin. "Yes sir, he telling you the truth. I'm sorry I worried y'all so bad."

Daddy clasped his hands over his vest. "You know all about the Bible, Annie, so I'm sure you know it says man cannot live by bread alone." Then he chuckled. "And Doctor Wall says a woman can't live on nothing but cornbread."

"Yes, sir," Dumah said. "I'd feel mighty bad if we done sent poor Annie off to the 'sylum and nothing ailing her but the wrong sumpn-to-eat."

"'Scuse me, Doctor," Annie said, "but you reckon I could make us a little pone of cornbread once in a while?"

"Once in a while, Annie, no more. By the way, will you all do me a favor?"

"Yes sir, we sure will," they said in chorus.

"On your way home stop by the jail, tell Sheriff Howell that Annie's feeling fine."

She shook her head. "Doctor, we don't mean no disrespect, but we don't want no parts of that jail. No parts of that sheriff, neither. He'll shoot you quick as look at you."

"Oh, don't go in," Daddy said. "Just knock at the door and pass a message for the sheriff, say Annie's feeling fine and won't need to go to the asylum after all. And tell him Dumah's able to get about his business again. Sheriff Howell will like that."

The pair exchanged glances, then Dumah said, "Since you the one asking us, Doctor, we'll do it. But don't neither one of us like that man."

Daddy didn't like him either, and he enjoyed sending Sid Howell a reminder of who'd had the upper hand.

As CHILDREN, Anne and I were taught a procedure for answering the phone: write down the time, the name, the phone number if there was one, and directions to the patient's home if required. On holidays, nights, and weekends, both colored and white would come to the side door of our house looking for Daddy, and if he decided to treat them in the small side room used for that purpose, Anne and I were sometimes allowed to watch and "help." We learned a lot about diagnosis and treatment—for simple injuries, "Soak it in water with Epsom salts" was a sure-fire cure.

We rarely sat down for a Thanksgiving or Christmas dinner without interruption by a call for his help. And no matter who was calling, Daddy never refused to go. He'd get up from the table, saying, "I wonder who's been shot today" (we lived in hunting heaven), or "It must be a wreck." He so loved to eat, however, that most of the time he quickly completed the meal before leaving to treat the patient. Rarely was he able to enjoy the long, lazy, holiday afternoons and get-togethers many other families knew.

With time and improvement in the economy, Daddy's practice continued to grow and more patients became able to pay. For me, one of the first clues to the upswing in our fortunes was the new train table and marvelous array of electric trains that materialized in my attic playroom. I didn't know, but Anne did, that Daddy had had the dickens of a time getting such a set for me during wartime, when metal toys were hard to find. He went all over the state in search of it before he succeeded. When it was all set up, tiny streetlights gleamed beside the tracks, crossing gates moved up and down, engines ran forward or reversed or switched onto one of the spurs. The bridges and overpasses seemed as real as real, the elaborate set-up replete with miniature houses and stations, bushes and trees.

Daddy had done all that for me, and playing with my trains was so much fun that I forgot about going everywhere with him. Day after day my buddy Charles Rice came over and we climbed the attic steps to enter a magical world. Charles and I must have run those trains a thousand miles. It was every boy's dream, and my super Daddy had made it come true.

EVEN SO, from time to time Daddy would still invite me to ride out with him in the car. One Sunday he and I were headed to Fort Gaines, where he'd been called to see a patient feared to have pneumonia.

"Daddy, what if you have to put him in the hospital?"

"Maybe I won't have to. This new penicillin ought to do the job."

"But what if it doesn't?"

"Then I'll send him to Dr. Patterson's hospital in Cuthbert." Although by that time Daddy had the biggest following in several counties, his patients needing hospital care went thirty miles away to Cuthbert or across the river to Dothan, Alabama, never to the local clinic Dr. Holland owned, known as Holland Hospital. When a specialist was needed, he might send a patient as far as Albany—fifty-two miles—or, more rarely, one hundred miles to Thomasville to be cared for by his distant relative, another Dr. Wall. Besides working a significant hardship on his patients, these limitations kept Daddy from doing many surgical procedures he was qualified to perform.

"One of these days, son," he said, "we'll have a modern hospital in Blakely, one that can serve the whole county. Oh, I know Price Holland runs that little clinic his daddy built, but we need a fully equipped general hospital that can take anybody.

"Right now, when a child needs a tonsillectomy, I have to do it in the office, then send him home as soon as the ether wears off and the bleeding stops. Just think how much better it would be if we had a sure-enough operating room where we could do any kind of operation, an emergency room, hospital beds where a patient could be nursed."

He always talked to Anne and me as if we were his peers, never talked down to us in the least. He'd decided we were both in training for a medical career and often told us so. Hundreds of times we observed him at work, asked questions later, and got a complete explanation. He delighted in supplying it, a natural teacher who loved children and was as wonderful with us as with all the rest.

"I bet one day you can make a hospital happen," I said.

"Who knows? Maybe we can."

I took serious note of that "we," confident that he looked forward to the day when I was a grown-up doctor myself and would join him in practice. Doctor Wall and Little Doc, working together. I couldn't imagine a higher goal.

EVERYBODY IN TOWN KNEW DADDY, and most of them liked him a lot. And as people will do with doctors, wherever he went they didn't hesitate to ask for medical advice.

Charlie Dunning's barbershop was one of the places local folks dropped in regularly, to feel the pulse of the town. In the back of the shop Charlie had a bathroom with a shower, and when farmers came to town and wanted to get cleaned up, he let them use it. Rural bathrooms were still uncommon, and many folks appreciated Charlie's.

One Saturday Daddy was in the barbershop having his hair cut when a local farmer he knew walked in, looking grim. I was reading a comic book, waiting for Daddy.

Daddy raised a hand in greeting. "Morning, Ervin. How're you doing?"

"Doc, I ain't worth a damn."

"What's the matter?"

The farmer shook his head. "I ain't taken a shit in a week."

"That sounds rough. Have you tried an enema?"

The farmer looked puzzled. "What's that?"

"Go next door to the drugstore," Daddy said. "Get the druggist to sell you an enema set and bring it back, and I'll show you."

Of course, the barber, all the other customers, and I were fascinated by this exchange. The farmer went on his errand while Charlie finished Daddy's haircut, shook out the sheet, and brushed him off. Daddy stood up and was paying Charlie when the farmer came back from the drugstore carrying a paper sack.

Daddy unbuttoned his shirtsleeves and rolled them up. "Come on, Ervin, bring your bag and follow me." He and the farmer retired and shut the bathroom door.

Out front you could have heard a gnat sneeze. Charlie turned off the baseball game on the radio, and the rest of us strained our ears for whatever happened next. Until something did, neither hell nor hurricane could have run anybody out of that shop. I knew all about the upcoming procedure from personal experience and felt downright sorry for Ervin. Daddy would be filling the rubber bag with warm soapy water, then he'd tell Ervin to drop his pants before he homed in with the business end.

At first there was silence, followed by a howl of protest. "Damn, Doc, you ain't gonna stick that thing UP MY ASS!"

Laughter swept through the front room as Ervin's protests grew louder by the second: "Whoa, now, Doc! Whoa! WHOA, I SAY!"

We were all holding our sides laughing, and I figured Daddy was laughing too. The only one not laughing was poor Ervin. In the end (no pun intended), the operation was a success, and the thin bathroom walls did little to muffle the eventual explosion and groan of relief that followed.

With Daddy around to apply the proper treatment, even a bellyache could turn into good fun, and most everybody except other local doctors appreciated his comical approach. Those doctors stood on their dignity, taking themselves far more seriously. One in particular, Dr. Jack Standifer, had two claims to fame. As he was quick to tell anybody, he was a third-generation MCG graduate, and he'd risen through Masonic ranks to become a Potentate in The Ancient Arabic Order of the Nobles of the Mystic Shrine. To Dr. Standifer, Masonic or Shrine doings were the most important concern in life—far more important than the practice of medicine.

Daddy always laughed to see him, driving off to some Shrine event wearing his tasseled red flowerpot hat. If word of Daddy's ridicule got back to Dr. Standifer, he probably resolved one day to even the score. One day, he'd get his chance.

I REMEMBER A MORNNG when I was quite young and Daddy was able to sit down with us to breakfast without interruption. I knew he'd been out on a late-night call, for I'd heard the phone ring long after we were in bed.

"Is something bothering you, Henry?" Mother poured his second cup of coffee.

He reached for a biscuit and buttered it. "Yes, I'd better tell you about it."

The person phoning had been Sheriff Howell. "Got a prisoner here that needs you, Doc. Come down to the jail right now."

He didn't ask Daddy to come—he *told* him. That was how Sheriff Howell did things. Daddy would have gone in any case, because he never refused anyone who needed his help.

Nobody was around when Daddy parked on the square in front of the jail. Even the mules and horses in the livery stable across the street were quiet. The night was moonless, and there was just enough illumination at the jail door to reveal a great deal of blood on the front steps and stoop.

Inside, four people sat around a table: Sheriff Howell, his deputy, the skinny jailer Daddy had pegged as a drunk, and a bail bondsman who was also a loan shark. Poker cards and chips lay scattered on the tabletop, and only the sheriff would meet Daddy's gaze. He was such a scrawny-looking guy that nobody would find him a threat unless they knew his reputation. You might have taken him for a country lawyer if you didn't know who he was. The usual cigarette stub drooped from a corner of his down-turned lips.

Daddy spoke first. "What's the problem, Sheriff? Seems like I saw blood on your front steps."

He had noticed another long smear of blood along the walkway that led to the cells, and when Howell stood up he saw more blood on the sheriff's tan pants.

"Niggers." The sheriff hitched up his belt and adjusted his Stetson, then shifted his cigarette to the other side of his mouth. "Damn drunk niggers got to fighting at a juke joint over on North Church. After the nigger that runs the joint called, I went out to see about it, and when one of the bastards thought he'd take me on, I had to cuff him to bring him in."

The other three men focused intently on counting the poker chips.

Daddy said, "Where's the prisoner you called me to see?"

Howell jerked his head in the direction of the cells. "Same nigger, back yonder in the lockup." From a nail on the wall he took down a big ring of keys, then motioned to Daddy. "Bring your bag and come on."

Daddy was following the sheriff when a cracked and callused hand grabbed him from between the first cell's bars. "Oh, Lord, Doctor Wall, I knowed that had to be you. You got to help me, get me out of this hellhole!"

It was a poor black farmer Daddy had treated for a septic cut.

"Why, Mose, how come they've locked you up?"

The man started to cry. "My God, Doctor Wall, you a good man, you got to get me outta here. All I done was steal two chickens, my chillun was starving, I couldn't stand it no more."

The sheriff had turned back. "What the hell?" He unholstered his gun and used it to prod the man back from the bars. "You got two seconds to shut up," he said.

Mose wrung his hands and backed off. "Doctor Wall, sir, please, can't you help me, lend me a little money or something? They liable to kill me!"

Howell called out, "Deputy, back here," and the uniformed man stood up from the poker table and came double-quick. "Here, take this loud-mouth nigger and put him in the holding cell where he can't bother anybody."

"Yes sir," the deputy said, unlocking the cell and jerking the prisoner out to handcuff him and lead him away. Silent but taking it all in, Daddy watched them go.

"Now I reckon we can get back to business," Howell said. Daddy followed along the otherwise empty cells, noticing a second holster on the sheriff's belt that held a blackjack matted in fresh gore. So much blood was smeared on the linoleum floor that he couldn't avoid stepping in it. Rank odors hung on the air: disinfectant, urine, yesterday's alcohol, vomit. The two men's footfalls, the creak of the sheriff's holsters, and the jangle of the keys were the only sounds.

The sheriff unlocked the last cell and flung the bars open to a gut-heaving scene. In a darkening pool of blood on the floor sprawled a black man, hands cuffed behind his back and one side of his head bashed in. Foul stains marked his trousers. The cell stank of the iron tang of blood, rotgut liquor, and shit.

Daddy knelt quickly to feel for a pulse, then stood up and frowned. "God almighty, Sheriff, this man's dead!"

"Hell yes he's dead. You write on that death certificate he had a heart attack."

Daddy glared at the corpse, then back at Howell. "Heart attack? Somebody beat this man to death. See these broken teeth, this head where it's battered in? And what about that blood on the steps, blood all the way from the front door?"

"That's none of your business. In fact, Doc, I see you got some blood on y'own pants, got some on your hands, too." The sheriff's mouth twisted. "Now, that doesn't look too good, does it? You better listen to me. I called you down here to see about this nigger. You say he's dead, can't do a thing for him.

"Well then, you just go on and write on that paper what killed him. Black sumbitch had a heart attack, hit his head when he fell. You write that down like I'm telling you, then you can go home."

"Sheriff Howell, you know this prisoner didn't have any heart attack. You're asking me to cover up a murder, and I'm not about to do it."

Howell's eyes narrowed to slits. "You young sawbones, I'm the law in this county. You'll do what I say—or else." His hand moved to his pistol butt. "And by God you better watch your mouth. Sumbitch is dead, all you have to do is put on that paper he died of *natural causes*."

Daddy picked up his medical bag and stood tall, and my daddy was then a very impressive man. "You can keep me here till Judgment Day if you want to, but you'll have to find some other doctor to cover up what you've done. Any paper I put my name to will state that this man died of a brutal beating to the head."

Sid Howell threw down his cigarette to squash it with his boot heel, then hooked both thumbs in his belt and squinted at Daddy for a long moment. His voice was ominous when he finally spoke.

"If you know what's good for you, Wall, you'll do as I say."

Daddy said, "When hell freezes over," and turned and walked out.

He had no difficulty working out the chain of events. Howell's violent reputation was well known, and his assailant had been sober enough to submit to the handcuffs rather than get shot. But on the way to the jail he'd been drunk enough to mouth off, and once there, some wrong move sealed his fate. Handcuffed and drunk, he couldn't defend himself, and Sid Howell beat him into oblivion on the outside steps.

After the beating, the sheriff or someone doing his bidding picked up the man's feet to drag him inside, his bloody head bouncing over the floor till they threw him into that last cell and left him to die. Howell hadn't bothered to remove the handcuffs or wipe his blackjack clean because he didn't give a damn. A dead black man could never testify, nor would the jailer, deputy, or bail bondsman take such a risk. No doubt they too remembered the hanging man. The only other witness, the terrified chicken thief, had been swiftly removed from the scene.

Daddy ended his story with a great sigh. "I drove home last night and walked in this house with my heart and my feet feeling like lead. I had to ask myself why, in this nice little town, would the full power of the law be entrusted to such a savage man? Hallie, do you think we made a mistake coming here?"

"I told you from the beginning we made a mistake when we passed through Albany and didn't settle there," Mother said. "We should have settled in Albany, not here. But the same thing could have happened anywhere in the South."

"I pray to the Almighty it couldn't," Daddy said, and when he stood up to leave for the office he must have seen how big my eyes were. Quickly, he sat back down to talk directly to me. "Now, son, I don't want you worrying or feeling scared for one minute. That sheriff's not going to bother you or me."

He shook a playful finger in my face and smiled. "If you live right, and do right—*which I'm sure you will*—you'll never have to worry about the so-called long arm of the law. Anyway, it's not all that long."

I shrugged and tried to act like I wasn't scared, but suddenly our little town no longer felt so safe. If Sheriff Howell would beat a helpless colored man to death, what might he do to the defenseless young son of the doctor who had defied him?

BY STANDING UP FOR WHAT WAS RIGHT, Daddy had made an enemy of a man as vindictive as he was brutal. In the weeks that followed, we started to hear of Sid Howell dropping in at country stores, gas stations, the barbershop, hardware store, anyplace people gathered, sounding off to one and all: "Y'all know that young doctor in town, Henry Wall?" Heads would nod. "Well, there's not a bigger nigger-lover around."

These were incendiary words in the South Georgia of those days. Sid Howell was setting out to ruin my daddy, and while many years would pass before he found the opportunity and the means, in the end he would fully succeed.

Chapter 3

Central to the pre–Civil Rights Solid South, Georgia was Democratic through and through. If you wanted to get elected, you ran as a Democrat no matter what. Eugene Talmadge, a populist lawyer, farmer, and mule-trader, had been elected to a two-year term as governor on the Democratic ticket in 1932, re-elected to another in 1934. He would be elected again in 1940, lose to young Ellis Arnall in 1942, and be re-elected in 1946, though he didn't live to take office. In my childhood, Talmadge's gangs had a power stranglehold in most county seats of the state, and Early County and Blakely were no exception.

While a Democrat himself, Gene Talmadge so bitterly opposed President Franklin D. Roosevelt and his New Deal programs that during his governorship in 1935, when FDR paid a visit to Georgia, the old fire-eater wouldn't even show up to welcome the President, saying he had business to attend to down on his farm. Daddy, on the other hand, traveled all the way to Gainesville in North Georgia to hear the President speak. Because Talmadge hated blacks and violently opposed to according black citizens their civil rights, any effort by President or Mrs. Roosevelt to accord the blacks greater opportunity evoked the old rabble-rouser's vituperation and hate. He meant for Georgia to have two citizen classes: whites, whose votes perpetuated his segregationist rule, and blacks too terrified to vote, whose rights were trampled.

Daddy was a Democrat, of course, but a fair and forward-thinking one, and over time he came to believe that as long as the Talmadge faction was in power, citizens of Georgia and of Early County in particular would know very little in the way of progress. Beyond Gene Talmadge's blatant racism, the reactionary governor ruled like a Caesar, never hesitating to fire anyone who opposed him and quickly filling the vacancies with his flunkies.

Georgia's voters could be persuaded for change, however, as the election of 1936 had shown. Eurith Dickinson "Ed" Rivers followed Talmadge in the governor's office from 1937 through 1940 and did an immense amount of good for the state's people. Governor Rivers supported President Franklin D. Roosevelt's economic recovery programs, worked for improvements in housing and public health, and promoted rural electrification. But toward the end of Rivers's term, as an economic crisis loomed and his influence ebbed, fiery old Gene Talmadge, smarting from two failed tries for the U.S. Senate, pawed at the ground.

The 1940 gubernatorial race brought the old campaigner charging out to run for office again, resurrecting his stock-in-trade racial war-cry. Talmadge won that election and proceeded to wreck the state's educational system, thanks to his violent feelings about "race-mixing"—the admission of black students to state-run, whites-only schools.

Daddy gritted his teeth and held on until the next election.

BECAUSE THE SNEAK ATTACK at Pearl Harbor happened before the advent of television, nobody in the continental U.S. viewed the horror live, but *Life* magazine was read avidly at our house every week, along with the Atlanta papers and the *Albany Herald*. After newsreel footage was dispatched to movie theaters everywhere, the black smoke billowing from crippled battleships became as familiar to Americans as the house next door.

Patriotic young men flocked to enlist. Daddy, eager to do his part, had to make a choice. A major's rank in the U.S. Army Medical Corps was his if he wanted it, or he could stay in Early County to provide medical care for farming families and anyone else left at home. A fervent patriot, he came up with a creative solution that filled both needs. He would carry on his practice and perform physical exams on draftees at no charge.

I soon noticed that sugar and eggs, butter and bacon were in short supply at our house. "Rationing," Mother said. "We have to give up some of our food so our country can feed the brave sailors and soldiers." I was cautioned not to be too hard on my shoes, because shoes were rationed

Early County Draft Board 1942.

along with lots of other things.

When I asked about the little blue-star flags I noticed in people's windows, Daddy said it meant a family member was in uniform. Soon my playmates and I, instead of playing cowboys and Indians, were digging foxholes in our backyards and playing war in our junior uniforms complete with helmets, badges, and wooden toy guns. "Banzai!" we would yell, or tear around the backyard hollering "Kill the Japs!" A hole remained in the backyard afterward for years.

As long as the old mule-trader stayed in the governor's mansion, Daddy and many other Georgians saw much that needed doing and knew Gene Talmadge wouldn't get it done. I didn't know much about politics, only that the name "Talmadge" brought frowns to faces in our house. But by late 1942, just five years old, I knew what was happening when Daddy's frustration with Talmadge turned to rejoicing. He couldn't stop talking about Ellis Arnall, what a fine man he was, how eager he was to see him elected governor. I would later learn that the idealistic young lawyer who had been Governor Rivers's attorney general seized on the educational debacle as the focus of his campaign to become Georgia's youngest governor ever.

Daddy told us Arnall had taken a stand against "ignorance, poverty, prejudice, hatred, and demagoguery." When I asked what all those big words meant, Daddy said, "Everything Gene Talmadge stands for." Arnall's rhetoric was music to Daddy's ears, and during the campaign he and Mother helped organize a barbecue on the courthouse square for their favorite candidate, with speeches, free food, and the like. And once the new governor took office, Daddy kept in close touch with him to let him know just how positive he felt about what he was trying to do.

Over the years to follow Daddy would frequently tell me about all the good things Governor Arnall had done. Right away he launched an ambitious program of statewide reforms, garnering widespread national press coverage. He did away with the political manipulations that had dogged the board of regents and university system. He eliminated the worst abuses in Georgia's prisons and abolished chain gangs on the state roads. Halfway through his term, he pressed for state constitutional reform. He fought to get the poll tax abolished. He was a segregationist like most of his class in those times but wise enough to realize that mono-racial voting must soon be swept away. In contrast to Gene Talmadge's two-class view, Governor Arnall acted on the belief that *every* Georgian was a first-class citizen.

These fresh winds of change stirred responsive chords in Daddy's soul. The remarkable new governor being praised across the nation was making life in Georgia better for nearly everybody. Daddy himself had persevered through medical school and had come to Early County for one reason only: to serve human need. So it was only natural that the positive new politics should eventually lead him to consider what more he himself might do.

The extended Wall family already had at least one model of public service. Daddy's admired uncle, John R. Wall, had represented his own district in the Georgia legislature and served for years as Schley County's tax commissioner. Daddy remembered that example and began to think that he might make some similar contribution himself. He had the personality for it in spades, plus an outstanding civic and professional reputation.

It was then the custom for our state senate seat to rotate among the three counties of the Ninth District—Baker, Calhoun, and Early—and with Early County's turn coming in 1944, Daddy began to think in earnest of running. He had a thriving medical practice and was enjoying his second term as president of the Blakely Rotary Club. And so, well aware of his local popularity and with encouragement from friends, he threw his hat in the ring.

At seven years old I was thrilled to see flyers with his pleasant face fluttering on telephone poles, posters featuring his big smile in store windows around the square. Daddy showed me the campaign advertisements in the newspaper and took me with him day after day as he crisscrossed the county in his car. We'd stop at country stores and crossroads so he could politick wherever a handful of people might gather. After all, he'd had plenty of practice.

"I'm Henry Wall," he'd say, sticking out that big beefy hand. "I'm a country doctor from Blakely, running for the state senate, and if you

W. H. Wall, Sr., with W. H. Wall, Jr., voting, 1946.

honor me with your vote, I'll do everything in my power to make things better for us all."

"Yes sir, Doctor Wall," his listeners would say. "You can count on us."

One of the proudest highlights of my young life came on Election Day. Daddy came into the kitchen that morning while I was having my cereal and bananas.

"Son," he said, "we're going down to the polling place today, and I want you to go with me. But I don't want you going down there in old or dirty clothes. In a free country like ours, voting is something special. So ask your mother to help you get dressed in your nicest clothes, the way you would for Sunday School—a white shirt and necktie—let her comb your hair nice and neat. Then I'll take you with me and let you drop my ballot in the slot."

That night after supper when the polls closed we all went down to stand around the courthouse while the votes were counted. It was a regular carnival atmosphere. People kept coming over to shake Daddy's hand. "Sure hope you get in, Doctor Wall." "Yessir, you got our vote." Daddy just kept smiling and nodding, basking in the good will. Sheriff Howell and his cronies were right there. I kept my eye on the sheriff the whole time, but he never came over to shake Daddy's hand.

The suspense mounted as returns from the rural precincts came in, and while the election was close, Daddy won. I was overjoyed. Thrilling times lay ahead. My daddy was a state senator, a big man now across the state as well as at home. I was sure everybody loved him, and even that scary sheriff would have to respect him now.

Many years later I would learn that the opposition camp had labeled Daddy "too liberal." For the times, that was probably the greatest compliment he could have had, because although in today's terms he would be considered a staunch conservative, he stood for everything the Talmadgeites opposed. He wanted progress for Georgia's people and believed everyone, including the blacks, deserved his fair share. The latter aspect of this view he had to hold close to his chest, for nobody voted in those days but white people, and speaking up for the blacks would have condemned him among the wool-hat boys. It was his popularity and the forward-thinking element among the voters that put him in office for that first two-year term.

WITH DADDY'S PRACTICE FLOURISHING, our family was modestly prosperous. A born optimist, he was proud to serve his state and believed he could afford the financial sacrifice required by going to the legislature. In terms of family expenses, Mother was the more conservative one, while Daddy always insisted that she shop for quality rather than waste money on cheap stuff. His size dictated custom-tailored suits and shirts, the latter always monogrammed like his handkerchiefs, and he had an array of fine hand-painted silk ties. Mother, on the other hand, shopped the sales and complained when he bought us gifts she considered too costly.

In a typical burst of generosity he bought me a beautiful Palomino mare named Princess—such a great source of pleasure that my pal Charles's and my interest in electric trains immediately waned.

My sister Anne got to go to sleep-away summer camp three years in a row. And Mother benefited from our improved fortunes with her own new car to drive, since Daddy needed his to travel to and from Atlanta. Gasoline and tires were still rationed, but as a physician he had always had an extra share. Even before wartime exigencies began to ease, life for the Wall family of Blakely, Georgia, was good, and we felt sure that whenever peace came, even better days lay ahead.

WE WERE ALL PROUD as could be in January of 1945 when Daddy set off to be sworn in for the 1945–46 senate term. While the legislature sat he expected to stay in an Atlanta hotel during the week. But because in our farming community Saturday had always been his busiest day for seeing patients, on Friday afternoons he would drive the 205 miles home over two-lane roads to be in the office bright and early the next day. We saw very little of him those weekends when he came home.

With Governor Arnall set to serve through 1946, Daddy quickly became a close friend and confidant of both the governor and Secretary of State Ben Fortson. The only physician in the legislature at the time,

GOVERNOR RECEIVES PETITION TO CALL EXTRA SESSION—Georgia Legislature leaders in the "Draft Arnall" movement present Governor Ellis Arnall with the
ion of 131 members of the House of Representatives and 35 members of the State
to call an extra session to amend the Constitution. Left to right are Ben Fort-
ted), Representative of Wilkes County; Lon Duckworth, chairman of the Dem-
te Executive Committee; Dr. W. H. Wall, senator from Blakely, Ga., and
Arnall.—Journal Photo.

Senator W. H. Wall with Gov. Ellis Arnall, Secretary of State Ben
Fortson, and Representative Lee Duckworth, circa 1946.

he agreed to serve as Governor Arnall's senate floor leader for the coming
two years—no small honor for a beginner in state politics.

He was particularly proud of being assigned to the committee to
revise Georgia's outdated constitution, even though it meant more time
spent away from his practice. The important task would be completed in
a record two months' time. Among its other provisions the new constitution, as approved and ratified, provided for the governor to serve one

four-year term but no immediate successive one. This particular provision would soon have far-reaching and unforeseen consequences.

If some matter came up to detain him in Atlanta, Mother, Anne, and I would take the train to join Daddy. Wartime passenger trains were so crowded that one might be thirty or forty cars long, jam-packed with so many servicemen and other travelers that many had to stand in the aisle. On one of those train rides a soldier was playing the harmonica. I was enthralled, and as we got off in Atlanta he gave me not one but two harmonicas to keep. I still have them.

To Anne and me, Atlanta was high cotton. Mother and Anne enjoyed shopping at Rich's or Davison's, finding things not available in Blakely or even in Columbus, the nearest big town. We always stayed at one of Atlanta's two first-class hotels—the Winecoff once or twice, but generally the Henry Grady. I still have a clear picture in my mind of the open stairwell that would contribute to the Winecoff's terrible December 1946 fire.

Back then every elevator had its uniformed and gloved operator, and at the Henry Grady they must have dreaded to see Anne and me coming. With Anne in charge of me, we were given the run of the hotel and entire block on which it sat. We got in those elevators and asked to be carried up and down, down and up, all over the hotel. We even went up on the roof to gape at the private penthouse. We'd go to one picture show, come out of it, and go straight into the one next door.

Whenever possible we'd go over to the capitol to watch the work of government being done, and I believed Daddy was the most important man on that senate floor. We covered the state museum on the top floor of the capitol thoroughly—knew every exhibit. Daddy introduced us to Governor Arnall, Secretary of State Fortson, and all sorts of celebrated folks.

When Anne noticed boys and girls scurrying around and asked Daddy who they were, he said, "Those are pages, honey. Would you like to be one?"

"Gosh, Daddy, could I?"

"Me, too!" I said.

Senators could sponsor a page for one week each term, and Daddy fixed it for both of us to skip school so we could serve as senate pages. I was underage for the role, but they made an exception and let us both serve. It was quite a change from playing GIs and Japs in a Blakely backyard.

DADDY'S FAMILY as well as his patients paid a price for his public service. State senators received twenty-five dollars a day while the legislature sat, plus a small allowance for mileage—not even enough to cover expenses, and certainly not enough to make up for the lost income. I was too young to grasp the full import, but Mother understood the cost all too well. The other Blakely doctors may actually have worked to get Daddy elected, because sending him out of town increased their own practice income.

The greater good was what always mattered to Daddy. Personal economic considerations took second place to politics, which was his energizer, the great joy of his life. By his side in a crowd, I was forever amazed at the way he drew people to him. He had an unforgettable presence, a palpable magnetism. Hale fellow well met, he always had a joke to tell, a personal detail to mention that endeared him to any acquaintance or friend. He was often described as "larger than life." Physically a big man, he had an equally big personality, and politics provided the perfect setting to exercise his talents and charm. His innate leadership ability and charismatic personality quickly made many friends for him and earned him widespread respect across the state. A letter written the following year suggests why:

Dear Doc:

I enjoyed your visit the other day very much and deeply appreciate your interest in my personal and political success. I esteem you very highly and want you to know that you can count on me always as your friend. I have always found that in my talks with you and my association with you I am pepped up over things in general more than with anyone else. If I can serve you at any time in any way, you know that the only thing necessary is to get in touch with me.

With best wishes, I am

Sincerely your friend,
Ben W. Fortson, Jr.
Secretary of State.

As Daddy's influence on the state level increased, our federal government was giving him well-earned commendations. During the war he volunteered far more patriotic service than the two other Blakely physicians—Dr. Holland and Dr. Standifer (Dr. Baxley was away in the military). By V-J Day Daddy had been awarded a Selective Service System medal "for faithful and loyal service," plus four Presidential citations—two signed by President Roosevelt, two by President Truman. Seeing that medal and those framed documents on his office wall thrilled me to my core. Two Presidents of the United States had actually written to my daddy—not once, but four times.

Beyond helping to revise the constitution, Daddy also was named head of the committee responsible for state colleges and hospitals. The job required travel all over Georgia and to contiguous states, often for several days at a time. At our dinner table when he came home after his first visit to the state mental hospital in Milledgeville he seemed disturbed, and Mother asked him what was wrong.

"Up at that hospital in Milledgeville there's a whole lot that's wrong," he said. "Really, it can hardly be called a hospital. I always assumed that those in charge were doing right by the patients, but I saw plenty up there today that needs to be set right."

He took up his fork, laid it down again, shook his head. "Those terrible wards—why, walking through them would break your heart."

I was struggling to imagine an insane asylum. "Do the people act real crazy?"

"Some do, son, but an awful lot of the folks are there for no other reason other than that their families won't have them. It's the saddest thing you can imagine. They might be retarded, or have some affliction such as cerebral palsy, or they might not have anything wrong with them at all except being poor and unwanted somewhere else. The place is a dumping ground, and it's a pathetic state of affairs."

Mother frowned. "If I were you, Henry, I wouldn't—"

"Hallie, these children are old enough to learn about such things. I want them to grow up aware of the need to make their world better. To begin with, there's not nearly enough staff, the wards are overcrowded, and most of what staff they have isn't adequately trained or qualified."

He shook his head, then took out his handkerchief to wipe his brow. "Demented patients walk around half-clothed, hallucinating, talking to themselves, and conditions in some of those wards are just unspeakable. We're having dinner, so I'll skip the details, but it's a snake pit. There's no other word for it." His eyes glistened.

I said, "If it's so bad, Daddy, can't you and those other men up in Atlanta fix it?"

"If I don't accomplish another thing in the senate"—he banged his fist on the table so hard we jumped, and the silverware danced—"that's one situation that *will* be addressed."

Daddy made good on his promise. He reported back to the legislature without mincing words, generating statewide publicity, and within a few months conditions at Milledgeville improved greatly. More staff were hired, dilapidated facilities were renovated, and training to improve care and services began. I was mighty proud of my dad. One day I meant to join him in helping people like that.

By the end of his first senate term he had accomplished a great deal. In addition to his help with the new constitution and the changes at Milledgeville, he pushed for sweeping statewide improvements in the detection and treatment of tuberculosis, made sure the Battey State Hospital at Rome was up to speed, and promoted free chest x-ray screening through new county health departments statewide. Today, thanks to those efforts, anyone in Georgia can still obtain a free chest x-ray exam at any county health department. Early County, like many others, opened its new public health department in 1946, with Daddy named its director—a consultant, primarily, or on call when required.

As our family had painful cause to know, malaria was another pressing problem, and he launched a program to wipe that out. At his urging, widespread DDT spraying was begun, and as mosquito havens

Above and right, Senator W. H. Wall inspecting Medical College of Georgia with Dr. G. Lombard Kelley, President, 1946.

were eliminated, malaria cases declined. If a family consented, their home was even sprayed free of charge, which had the added benefit of eliminating bedbugs. Unfortunately, the insecticide's detrimental effects were not then known, so Daddy endorsed the solution he believed best at the time. Had he known otherwise, of course he would have sought some other approach.

In concert with his old friend Dr. Kelley, now dean at MCG, Daddy had asked the 1945 legislature to consider funding a new four hundred-bed teaching hospital at MCG. Both men anticipated passage by the U.S. Congress of the Hill-Burton Act, to provide federal grants to upgrade medical facilities nationwide. A new hospital at MCG would surely qualify for such a grant. When the time came to open Georgia's door to Hill-Burton Act funds, Daddy helped Governor Arnall push the necessary legislation through. Although the legislature put off authorizing the new MCG facility, Dr. Kelley and Daddy held on to their vision.

By THE SPRING of 1945 it sank in with Governor Arnall's supporters that the new constitution didn't allow a popular governor to succeed himself, so Ben Fortson and Daddy launched a "Draft Arnall" movement. They hoped to pass an amendment allowing a successive four-year term for the widely admired incumbent, as well as any deserving future one. Strong pressure was brought to continue Governor Arnall's far-reaching programs, and Daddy and Ben led the charge.

"The people everywhere are afraid of a return to dark days in Georgia if the governor does not run again," *The Atlanta Journal* quoted Daddy as saying.

But neither Governor Arnall nor his wife—who had given birth to a baby girl while he was in office—were eager for a second term, and Arnall was already planning an extensive, highly remunerative lecture and book tour when he left office. Ammunition against the proposed amendment included Governor Arnall's own lukewarm interest in it, plus rank-and-file Talmadgeite resentment for his efforts to eliminate both the white primary and the poll tax.

Enough signatures to consider the amendment were obtained to convene a special session of the legislature, but when it took place in January of 1946 the Talmadge faction had mustered sufficient resistance to defeat the plan by eleven votes. Governor and Mrs. Arnall may not have grieved, but the defeat came as a great disappointment to Daddy and like-minded Georgians. The setback would have been even more painful had they known it marked Ellis Arnall's swan-song on the state's political scene.

In many ways Daddy's second year in the senate was pivotal. He had been under such terrific pressures in the political arena that he failed to recognize the onset of a condition undermining his own health. Physicians are notorious for taking better care of their patients than of themselves, and Daddy was no exception. A man who had always loved to eat, he now weighed nearly three hundred pounds, smoked over two packs of cigarettes a day, and drank coffee like it was about to be rationed again. Mother worried, but her worry didn't change his ways.

The first hint of trouble came when his chronically inflamed gums began to draw away from his teeth. It was periodontitis, and if his teeth were to be saved he would have to undergo a lengthy and excruciating form of treatment. He didn't yet suspect the underlying cause. The second hint came after he struck his shin on the footrest of his examining table and produced an ulcer that wouldn't heal. As the ulcer kept getting larger and deeper Daddy just put up with it, focusing on what seemed to him more important matters.

One morning when he headed out of the Henry Grady Hotel, using a cane, the doorman said, "Morning, Senator, I see you still hobbling. Ain't that sore leg got well yet?"

Daddy tried to laugh it off. "Nobody up here in Atlanta to nurse me."

"Put you a poultice on it, then, but for Lord's sake don't go to none of them doctors. They don't do nothing but tell you take two aspirins and call back tomorrow. I tell you, Senator, them doctors liable to kill you!"

Daddy enjoyed repeating the story, but the ulcer ate away until it was down to bone. Ordinarily an astute diagnostician, he failed to diagnose his own dangerous condition. Finally he consulted Atlanta internist Dr. Hal Davison and the diagnosis was made. It was Type II diabetes mellitus, not uncommon in overweight people, and Daddy was seriously overweight. Doctor Davison's prescription was sweeping: insulin injections, no nicotine or caffeine, shed a hundred pounds. The insulin was essential, but the latter two injunctions were more than Daddy could take. Doctor Davison also dictated in emphatic language that Daddy must take a half day off every week and four more weeks' vacation during the year—two in the summer and two at some other time. Daddy thought such "idleness" could be postponed.

He was enjoying happier thoughts, for he had in mind a grand project that would realize a long-standing dream. He resolved to build that modern hospital he'd talked about for Blakely, an up-to-date facility ready for his return to full-time practice at the end of his senate term.

He was thinking big, for Early County had a population of just over twenty thousand. He bought a suitable piece of property and hired an architect to draw up plans for a capacious one-story brick building, invested most of his own savings in the project, and applied for a loan from the Reconstruction Finance Corporation to cover the rest. Thoroughly familiar with the Hill-Burton Act's stringent specifications, he resolved that his new hospital would exceed every one.

In February, Governor Arnall wrote him this letter:

> Now that the legislature is over, I want to take time to write you and tell you personally just how very much I appreciate you and your friendship. You have made an excellent senator. You are a loyal friend. One of the very brightest spots in my administration has been your unfaltering and unswerving support. This is appreciated more than you will ever know, and your friendship is reciprocated fully . . .
>
> When you are in Atlanta, I hope you will come to see me.
>
> With highest personal regards and every good wish for your continued welfare and success, I am

Sincerely your friend,

Ellis Arnall

Governor

Rather than take off more time from work, Daddy had assumed two more major responsibilities. As his term ended, Governor Arnall had appointed him to the Georgia Board of Medical Examiners—the body charged with licensing physicians and taking disciplinary action against any who violated laws or professional ethics. More Atlanta meetings, more travel, more stress.

Beyond that, he accepted a three-year appointment as head of the State Hospital Authority, responsible for the asylum at Milledgeville. A great many balls to keep in the air, yet in public service Daddy was never a man to say no. The good horse seemed eager to work himself to death. Meanwhile the painful periodontal surgery went on.

As it happened, four years earlier, in April of 1942, *The New York Times* had carried an article headed "New Pain-Killer Is Found" about trials of a new synthetic, non–habit-forming, pain-killing drug named Demerol. The findings were described by a researcher at Winthrop Chemical Company (manufacturer and distributor of the drug), a physician at New York University College of Medicine, and two staff physicians at the U.S. Public Health Service Hospital for Narcotic Drug Addicts in Lexington, Kentucky. These four medical professionals declared that Demerol (meperidine) "may be the long-sought substitute for morphine."

In September of the following year, *Newsweek* had carried a similar piece headed "Drug Without Addicts," quoting the same researchers' claim in the *Journal of the American Medical Association* that "dependence on Demerol has not yet been encountered in 'normal' (non–drug-addicted) persons."

That same year, however, the *United States Dispensatory* warned that the drug "can cause addiction"—a warning few physicians would have seen.

In spite of this quiet early red flag, three years later the June 1946 *Reader's Digest* featured an article by controversial bacteriologist Paul de

Kruif, Ph.D., entitled "God's Own Medicine." Doctor de Kruif touted Demerol and repeated the same non–habit-forming claim. Both *Time* and *The New York Times* promptly ran strong warnings to practitioners and the public to ignore de Kruif's glowing endorsement.

But it was too late for thousands who had already welcomed its relief. When it was first hailed as a revolutionary discovery, many physicians began prescribing Demerol with enthusiasm, while plenty of others had their doubts. Also in 1946, at the A.M.A. Convention, Federal Narcotics Commissioner H. J. Anslinger reported known cases of addiction to the drug and predicted a nationwide "wave of Demerol addiction" unless physicians took a stand against de Kruif's "reckless and dangerous" claims.

Whether Daddy or the medical men looking after him ever read or heard of these warnings we have no way to know. Miserable with both his teeth and his bum leg, he simply welcomed his first Demerol prescription as a godsend. Whether it was his periodontist or Dr. Davison who wrote that script we don't know either, and it makes no difference. The drug gave Daddy sufficient relief to get on with his considerable burden of work, which was all that mattered to him.

ELLIS ARNALL WAS ON THE WAY OUT, and the old "Wild Man" Gene Talmadge was by then a very sick man. Yet Talmadge was so determined to reclaim his power base that he ran again on the Democratic ticket for governor—and, as election time drew near, resorted to Ku Klux Klan involvement to keep blacks from the polls. This time, unfortunately, he found plenty of support.

I was only nine years old, but I vividly remember how embarrassed I felt listening to his stump speech on Blakely's courthouse square. Daddy and I were both there, and I knew almost everybody in the large, mostly white crowd. For some reason two black doctors from Bainbridge had come to the rally and stood unobtrusively at the back of the crowd. Heedless of possible criticism, Daddy went over to speak to them and shake their hands. His critics didn't care that these were his fellow physicians and educated men. In South Georgia in those days a white man wasn't supposed to shake hands with a black man. Knowing those two doctors were there hearing Talmadge rant about "niggers," I just squirmed. How awful to hear yourself referred to with such scorn!

I wasn't the only one who didn't like it. The barefoot son of one of Daddy's white patients stood near me as this diatribe ended, and when old Mr. Talmadge came down grinning from the platform and walked by, he patted this boy on the head.

"Now then, sonny, you be sure to tell all your family to vote for me."

The boy stuck his hands in his overall pockets and rared back so he could look Mr. Talmadge in the eye. "No, sir. I'll not tell 'em no such a thing. I ain't old enough to vote, but if I was, I wouldn't vote for you if they run a nigger against you."

My druggist friend Bob Hall will never forget Election Day. "All excited, I had caught a ride to town with a colored man driving a cotton wagon, and people were flocking toward the square. I said to the driver, 'I reckon you're going in town today to vote.'

"That colored man just gave me a long look, and I was really puzzled. So I said it again. 'It's Election Day, aren't you going to vote?' He looked at me with this world-weary expression, and it was only when he let me off on the courthouse square and I saw the voters lining up that I understood. The only people going to the polls in Blakely were white. I've thought about that experience many times. I was just a boy, but it showed me how wrong that state of affairs was, and I knew it had to change."

Next day the *Albany Herald* carried the election returns.

"Well, Hallie," Daddy said, "it's back to the Dark Ages. The old buzzard has done it again."

Mother explained that Mr. Talmadge, sick as he was, had won. But he had not yet been sworn in when, just before Christmas, he died. The 1945 constitution had introduced the office of lieutenant-governor, elected independently of the governor, to replace any sitting governor who could not serve, but Talmadge wasn't "sitting." In their haste, the revisers had overlooked any provision for a governor-elect who might die before being sworn in. No one could recall such an event.

So the great question arose: who was Georgia's governor? Nobody was sure. After Daddy went back to Atlanta, Mother tried to explain it to me, but the puzzle was enough to stump a hundred lawyers. Melvin Ernest Thompson had been elected lieutenant-governor, but he was not yet *actual* lieutenant-governor. Governor Arnall, Daddy, and the rest of their faction contended that Thompson should step up to become governor and fought hard to promote their view.

Naturally the Talmadgeites rebelled, demanding that the general assembly decide. They based their demand on a provision in the constitution stating that if an elected governor could not serve, the legislature would choose the new governor by deciding between the two general-election candidates garnering the second and third highest number of votes. Plenty of voters must have figured old Gene wasn't long for this world, because more than eight thousand had cast write-in votes, with 675 of those reported for Herman Talmadge, the old man's Navy veteran son. And those 675 write-ins were enough to win—provided the legislature had the right to elect anybody.

The battle that followed was bitter. Governor Arnall, still acting in his official capacity, convened a tabulating committee to recount the write-ins, and the Talmadgeites were stunned when the committee reported that young Herman had actually come in not first or second, but *third.* It looked as if he couldn't become governor after all, until the delegation from Telfair County—the Talmadge stronghold—raised loud objections and quickly produced another fifty-eight votes "incorrectly placed in the wrong envelope." That number was just enough to keep the Talmadge dynasty afloat.

So, on January 15, 1947, the strongly Talmadgeite legislature elected Herman Talmadge to a four-year term as governor, and most people thought that was that.

But it wasn't, not quite. Daddy's close friend and ally, wheelchair-bound Ben Fortson, had the duty of affixing the state seal to all election results, and wily Ben hid the seal under his chair's seat to avoid making the election official. Daddy was disappointed, expecting young Talmadge

Gov. Herman Talmadge's inauguration, 1948. W. H. Wall is visible
over Talmadge's left shoulder.

to be a chip off the old block; nevertheless, Ben's stunt provided a good
laugh.

Undeterred, Herman Talmadge took the oath of office and gave
his inaugural address, after which matters went from bad to worse. The
Talmadgeites marched on Governor Arnall's capitol office and broke
down the outer doors, intending to put Herman in his "rightful" place,
then marched on the Governor's Mansion, aiming to evict the Arnalls.
The national press quickly caught the scent of another great joke at
Georgia's expense.

Challenged by Governor Arnall as the "pretender," young Talmadge
nevertheless began to act as governor, while Governor Arnall was forced
to set up a separate office elsewhere in Atlanta. Three days later, after
M. E. Thompson was sworn in as lieutenant-governor, Governor Arnall
immediately resigned to allow Thompson to become governor, while
Herman clung to his position like a tick on a bird dog.

In the days that followed, newspapers all over the state blared protests
of the Talmadge faction's dubious and high-handed procedures. Ministers,
editors, writers, students, and citizens of every sort raised their voices to

condemn what they called an unlawful seizure of authority. Comparisons were made with Nazi tactics and Hitlerism. Mass meetings were held to register public disapproval, anti-Talmadge petitions were signed. The national press had a field day with the "three governors" dispute.

The contesting factions petitioned the Georgia Supreme Court to decide the matter, and Arnall, before he left on a national speaking tour, satisfied himself by a quiet inquiry that the high court would rule in Thompson's favor. Then, a few days before the court was to hear the case, *The Atlanta Journal* made national headlines with its report of investigations into those suspicious Telfair County write-in votes. Atlantans got it as front-page news, the paper reporting that one precinct had recorded 103 write-in votes, some of the alleged voters being dead, and the last thirty-four having voted "in alphabetical order." This laughable revelation must have carried at least a little weight with the high-court justices as the time to decide drew near.

The resolution finally came on March 19, when the court ruled as Governor Arnall had expected, in favor of Thompson and against Herman Talmadge's claims. At that point Talmadge, after serving sixty-three days as putative governor, had the good sense to accede to the court's ruling and step down.

If Daddy ever had a political idol, Ellis Arnall was the man, and a worthy one at that. Having Thompson as the new governor wasn't such a bad thing, but for Daddy, seeing his friend Ellis buffeted by such a storm of conflict and a return of the old demagogic buffoonery was more than he could take. He feared the wave of progress for Georgia might be at a standstill, and the donnybrook left him feeling sad and disgusted.

So for a while he was relieved to bid politics farewell and return home. The whole affair had been a great strain. Even when he came back to take up his old starring role in my life again, he still had far too much on his plate—taking care of his health, attending to the new hospital's completion and management, serving on the Board of Medical Examiners, overseeing the hospital at Milledgeville, and all that on top of full-time medical practice. Sooner or later something was bound to give.

Chapter 4

Daddy's excitement was contagious as the walls of Blakely's new hospital rose. Mother took time off from PTA and other community affairs to help a little with plans for the kitchen and furnishings.

Late every afternoon I'd go down to the construction site and walk among the partitions, picturing the hospital complete—shining floors, gleaming instruments in their cases, grateful patients recuperating in their brand-new adjustable beds. And Daddy in charge of it all. He was constantly making lists and researching every item needed, all the way from the finest windows Andersen made and doors wide enough to push beds through, to durable flooring materials, towel bars, and waiting-room chairs.

One afternoon I stopped by as the electricians were packing up after a long day and Daddy came in to check on the day's progress.

"Hey, there, son, how you doing? Isn't this looking fine? Come with me to the operating room a minute, I want to show you something."

I followed, making my way through a maze of cardboard cartons.

He pointed to the operating-room ceiling, then laid an arm across my shoulders. "You see that light? That's a Castle light, the finest available from American Hospital Supply. That light alone cost as much as a new Buick automobile, and the operating table that goes under it is costing every penny as much."

"Great day in the morning!" I couldn't imagine such costs.

"I tell you, son, from now on we won't have to take a back seat to anybody."

"What kinds of operations will you do in here?"

"Tonsils and adenoids like always, but with a much better set-up.

And I'll be able to do appendectomies, nail broken hips and legs, repair hernias, patch up stab and gunshot wounds. We see an awful lot of farm injuries, you know, and now I'll be able to really fix those up, even do the female surgery I've been referring out. Not a single patient should have to go out of town for care."

"Gosh, Daddy, that's great."

He guided me across the hall to another room. "Now, you see, this is our labor and delivery suite. We'll deliver babies in here. I've ordered the last word in equipment for these rooms too. I mean for Wall Hospital to be the most modern in South Georgia."

"Wall Hospital? Not Blakely Hospital?"

He shook his head. "No sirree. Wall Hospital, in memory of your grandmama and granddaddy Wall." Suddenly his eyes got even brighter. "Say, that gives me a great idea. We'll invite everybody in town to furnish rooms here in memory of their own folks." He pulled out a pocket notebook to jot down his idea, and by the time Anne was home from sleep-away camp and the hospital was open, all twenty-eight rooms had been completely furnished by donor friends.

DADDY'S PRIDE in his creation was so great, it never occurred to him to bring in somebody to handle the management side. He believed he could cover all the bases, because he'd always been so good at what he did—his first serious mistake.

To Daddy's way of thinking, he was already doing well financially and would do even better once the hospital got going, thanks to the additional surgical fees. Our house was paid for, and his fee for an office visit had risen to the grand sum of $3.00—$5.00 if you needed a penicillin shot. He and Mother lived carefully, never extravagantly, rarely taking a vacation or time off, and over the previous decade and a half of fourteen-hour days he had saved up nearly $70,000 in the bank.

In the end the hospital project came in at about $130,000—big money in 1947. He plowed every cent of his savings into the new hospital and agreed to make monthly payments on an RFC loan for the rest. When the time came to pay his federal income tax, the reserves simply weren't

Wall Hospital, 1948.

there. So Daddy put off paying the Internal Revenue Service—his second serious mistake.

He and his own doctors, along with thousands of other Americans, had already made another serious mistake—accepting Winthrop Chemical's early claims that Demerol was a non–habit-forming drug. Despite the ongoing periodontal treatment Daddy would eventually lose all but three of his teeth, and throughout that lengthy and painful ordeal he relied on the painkiller to keep going. Warnings about the drug were now broadcast widely, and Winthrop Chemical dropped its false claims, but for Daddy it was too late. He was hooked and forced to safeguard the most terrible secret of his life.

At last the big day for Wall Hospital came. Five nurses, a cook, and a secretary-treasurer made up the staff. Daddy presided over the grand opening, welcoming local folks who came to admire the new facility and wish him well. Refreshments were served. Potted plants and congratulatory flower arrangements banked the waiting room, including a tribute from Mayor Mack Strickland and the Blakely City Council.

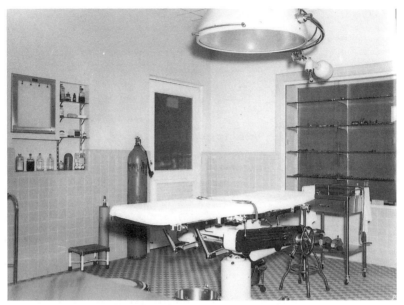

Wall Hospital Operating Room, 1948.

My buddies Jay Gandy and Charles Rice lined up with me and the other visitors to sign the guest book. Daddy, even happier than usual, welcomed everybody, beaming like Santa Claus. At last Early County had the modern hospital he'd dreamed of during all those years of practicing in cramped space with facilities that limited his skills. Now he had an emergency entrance, a proper labor and delivery suite, a bona fide operating room with every instrument in the book, fully equipped examining rooms, and comfortable quarters for patients both white and colored who needed hospital care. For his own office he had brought in a massive mahogany desk that immediately became one of his proudest possessions.

At suppertime I wanted to hear him voice his own excitement, say how truly pleased he was. "This sure has been a big day, Daddy, hasn't it?"

"A wonderful day." His smile was as warm as a South Georgia sun. "A lot of water over the wheel since we came to Blakely to start out."

Mother started the bowl of butterbeans around the table. "I suppose the other local doctors came by to congratulate you."

Daddy gave her a quizzical look. "Do you really suppose that?"

"I know you invited them. Surely one or two came."

We waited through a long silence till Daddy shook his head and let out a big, slow breath.

"No, Hallie. Not a single one."

In the weeks that followed, however, plenty of other visitors came. Daddy was showing two Atlanta surgeons the new operating room and almost burst his buttons when he heard one tell the other, "Don't you wish we had a room like this at Grady?" Grady—the biggest hospital in Atlanta!

To my considerable envy, Anne was soon pressed into service at the hospital. It was volunteer service, but there she was, a sort of nurse's aide taking temperatures and pulses, adjusting beds, answering the call button and relaying patients' needs to the nurses. I longed to work there myself, but Daddy said ten years old was too young.

"You be patient, son. Your time will come." I clung to that hope as tight as the bark on a Georgia pine, glad enough to be passed over when I learned that Anne and Mother were also having to shell peas and but-terbeans, or peel peaches and pears along with the kitchen staff. I wanted to be a doctor, not a kitchen maid.

With his new hospital serving a four-county area of Georgia and parts of eastern Alabama, Daddy's reputation continued to spread. He invited other local doctors to admit patients to Wall Hospital; none of them did. With the increased demands on his time and energy he soon saw the need for an associate, so on his next trip to Atlanta he interviewed young doctors completing their training. At Grady he found his man, and six months after Wall Hospital opened, Dr. John McLeod finished his surgical residency and came to join Daddy in practice.

Right away Dr. McLeod began assisting in surgery. In the months that followed, the operating-room log mentioned other occasional as-sistants: Drs. Cook, Gamble, Rhyne, Culbreth, and Newman, Daddy's medical-school roommate Dr. Herman "Dick" Dismuke from Ocilla, and Dr. Baxley, the only local man, now back from the war. I knew Daddy considered Dr. Baxley the best qualified of the town's other doctors, yet his name appears in that log book only once. When Dr. McLeod wasn't assisting, one of the nurses on staff did.

Most of Daddy's surgical skills had been dormant for fourteen years, yet once the hospital provided a suitable setting, he began operating again—major surgery, in many cases—with confidence and excellent results. While he most enjoyed obstetrics and orthopedics, he took on a wide range of cases. Reading that surgical log amazes me: tonsillectomy and adenoidectomy, repair of phimosis, hysterectomy, dilatation and curettage for incomplete abortion (miscarriage), removal of bladder and prostate tumors, surgery for perforated ulcers, removal of ovarian cysts, repair of various kinds of motor-vehicle trauma, and setting or pinning fractures of the hip, arm, leg, or foot. He brought a doctor 150 miles from Macon to operate successfully on two patients with broken necks and he himself provided the aftercare. Today every one of those operations is performed by a highly specialized surgeon.

Even more astonishing, he was doing major abdominal surgery with no type and cross-match available for blood transfusions, although a condition such as a perforated stomach ulcer can bring on tremendous bleeding. Nor did he have a comfortably air-conditioned operating room in which to work. Air-conditioned buildings weren't heard of in those days, and summers in South Georgia can be fiendishly hot. Many times after I grew old enough to help, I stood at his side while he operated and reached up to mop his dripping brow.

Before the hospital opened Daddy had undertaken postgraduate work on spinal anesthesia, to make sure he performed it correctly. At other times anesthesia was administered by local or regional injections, or by ether drip. When ether was used Daddy always put the patient to sleep himself, then had his assistant carry on with the drip till he was through. When I began to help out in the hospital a few years later, I could always tell when ether had been used, because the odor would leach through the recovering patient's skin to permeate the place.

Deliveries by other Blakely doctors had been known to lead to birth injuries, but none of Daddy's ever did. By the end of his career he had delivered more than two thousand babies without a single birth injury, and very few of those cases were Caesarean sections. How many obstetricians today can say the same? While my memories are naturally tinged with filial pride, no one can question the truth that Daddy was, by any measure, an extraordinary physician.

A COLORED FAMILY who brought their horribly burned toddler to the hospital provided Daddy with one of his most dramatic and challenging cases. Little Forestine's injuries were so severe they sickened everyone who saw her. Today she would be sent to the Shriners' Burn Hospital, but if that option was available then, I don't believe it was ever considered.

Her mother had been boiling clothes in an outdoor washpot when Forestine fell in the fire, to be seared over most of her body. Burns over more than fifty percent of a person's body were then believed to be fatal, and Forestine's burns over legs, arms, and abdomen were more extensive than that.

The prospect of caring for her was a sobering one. Months, maybe even years of treatment would be required, and the family hadn't a dime. Daddy admitted the baby to the hospital anyway and began plotting out skin grafts to be taken from her back, the only thing that would save her. The nurses, the cook, the regular receptionist, Anne, the whole staff of the hospital quickly fell in love with the little girl. During periods when she wasn't confined to her crib, the hospital staff taught little Forestine to walk again, toddling in her diaper, as they held her two hands.

Eventually her grafts "took" to the point that Daddy let her family carry her home, only to bring her back a short time later with a massive infection. He was furious. The mother had taken the child to a backwoods "witch doctor," who rubbed ashes into the healing wounds. Back to the hospital Forestine came for another long spell of care.

For quite a long time Daddy and the nurses looked after her faithfully until she was well enough to go home again, yet Daddy knew that the home situation was no more favorable than before. Once she left the shelter of the hospital, all his hard work and attentive care could quickly be undone. He had become so attached to her and had such hopes for her, in fact, that he floated a radical suggestion at home:

"Hallie, I think we ought to adopt little Forestine."

For the first time in my life I saw Mother speechless with shock.

He turned to my sister. "Anne, what do you think of the idea?"

Almost as speechless at Mother, she finally shook her head and said, "Daddy, you can't! I don't think that would work."

I certainly couldn't picture myself with a little colored sister. We knew how fair-minded Daddy was in racial matters, but this was going too far. In 1940s small-town South Georgia, such an idea could not have been more extreme.

"Now, Henry, you listen to me," Mother said. "I've gone along with you every way I can, but I'll go to my grave before I'll adopt Forestine or any other black child! No indeed, not while there's breath in my body."

Daddy was usually in charge, but not this time. Why he even entertained such an arrangement mystified me. I was just a kid, and even I knew it wouldn't work. Eventually Forestine went home, and I hope she's had a good life. This much I know—she survived her injuries only because of Daddy's generous heart, medical expertise, and gratis extended care.

BEYOND DADDY'S FAILED PLAN to adopt Forestine, Mother was worried in another, more pressing way. In the past, whenever she'd needed money for clothes, groceries, whatever, she'd asked Daddy and he'd provided. Now, with our personal finances and the hospital finances hopelessly intermingled, most of our family's resources were going into running the hospital. We didn't have as much to live on as before, and Mother tried to make Daddy see that hospital costs were outpacing the income from it.

Medicare and Medicaid hadn't been thought of, and Early County was still far from prosperous.

"You have to be careful about spending too much," she said. "Watch what goes out, and watch what comes in."

Daddy wasn't exercised about it. In the course of their practice most doctors expected to provide a certain amount of charity care, and he went far beyond the average. We'd all heard him say, "I've never sued a patient for non-payment, and I never will."

Mother told him that far too many accounts were being written off, and statements to patients rarely went out on time. It was a lost cause. Quibbling over money just was not Daddy's way. For years I'd gone with him on house calls, and the routine was always the same. I stood to one side while Daddy talked with the family and treated the patient, never a word said about fees. Rarely, when he was leaving and the patient or a family member asked what they owed, Daddy would just say, "I'll get the office to send you a bill." But if the patient or family didn't mention it, neither did he. He seemed downright embarrassed to mention payment; I think he considered talk of money a contamination of the doctor-patient relationship. When he died, twenty years after Wall Hospital opened, accounts receivable stood at more than a quarter of a million dollars, and very little of it was ever paid.

I WAS THIRTEEN YEARS OLD when Princess, my Palomino mare, died. A fungus had gotten into some damp feed, and the consequences were swift and horrible. Within hours she had the blind staggers and quickly died a miserable death.

I was heartbroken, and felt responsible because I'd let the feed get damp.

Daddy knew I'd always wanted to follow in his footsteps; now I needed something to console me for my painful loss. Anne was working at the hospital. Could I come in too? Daddy agreed and set me to running errands, mopping floors, and running the big rotary polisher over the asphalt tile—doing orderly work, any job that didn't require a registered nurse. I didn't get paid. I was just thrilled to have the opportunity and Daddy's trust.

After he saw how quickly I caught on, he even took me with him into the operating room, at first to stand at his side and keep him from dripping sweat. I soon advanced to another, more important job, relieving the nurse-assistant for other duties. If I was helping out when he put a surgical patient to sleep with ether, he took pains to teach me how to continue dripping the anesthetic until the operation was done. It wasn't complicated, and I was hugely proud of my new skill.

"You know, son," he said with a grin, "putting them to sleep isn't hard. The crucial thing is waking them up." I didn't worry, because Daddy was there to see that everything went as it should. It never occurred to me that letting a thirteen-year-old administer anesthesia might be more than a tad unwise—especially a thirteen-year-old who'd recently brought about his cherished mare's death.

Decades later, when I was in postgraduate oral-surgery training and being taught the use of ether, I was sorely tempted to blurt out, "Hey, fellows, giving ether is duck soup. Why, I was doing this when I was thirteen!" Nobody would have believed me.

AN ALABAMA FAMILY who'd heard about Daddy traveled more than a hundred miles to see him, bringing their skeletal infant and a laundry basket heaped with medications prescribed by other doctors. That baby looked to me exactly like pictures of starving prisoners in the Nazi concentration camps. Without hesitation Daddy diagnosed pyloric stenosis—a narrowing between the stomach and small bowel. The projectile vomiting associated with the condition quickly brings on malnutrition, so that without proper treatment, most afflicted babies die within weeks. This child, already near death, was too feeble to survive a general anesthetic, so Daddy performed the major surgery under *local* anesthesia for a complete cure.

Yet as I learned more and more of what went on in the hospital and Daddy's practice, I began to feel uneasy about certain things. Always an excellent organizer and planner, prepared for every eventuality, Daddy seemed to be growing neglectful. He got careless about paying bills and would never watch the difference between money coming in and money going out. He just wanted to help everybody get better, regardless of the cost. When Mother tried to correct the situation, he brushed her off. Tension between them rose, and all of us felt the fallout.

When Anne and some of her high school friends were injured in a car crash, Anne was taken to Wall Hospital for treatment. Doctor McLeod was attending her, and when Daddy came in, at first he didn't recognize his own daughter. They got her patched up and kept her for a few days. One day when Mother came down to check on her she saw something that sent her into a fury. I never knew what it was, but she raised the roof and demanded to carry Anne home to look after her there.

The discovery, whatever it was, had so disturbed Mother that from that point on she began going to the hospital every day to oversee the business: sending out bills, supervising collections, trying to bring order into Daddy's slipshod finances. While she'd never done any other work than teaching music, she was a good organizer and did her best to improve the balance sheet. After all, our livelihood depended on the hospital's financial success. Mother even became the first Blue Cross/Blue Shield agent in the area, hoping that if people bought the insurance more of their bills would get paid.

"THEY'RE GETTING up a new tennis team at school," I told Daddy when I was fourteen. "I really want to go out for it, but I don't have a racquet. Can you get me one?"

"Sure," he said. "Come by the office this afternoon when school lets out."

Visions of that fine racquet of Anne's tantalized me. It had cost twenty-five or thirty dollars, not cheap, but I was sure Daddy would get me one just as good, because he always wanted us to have the best of everything. Promptly at four o'clock I showed up at his office, ready to ride to Dothan.

"Let me finish up with this last patient," he said, "then we'll go."

When we got in the car he didn't take the road to Dothan but drove straight to the Western Auto store right there in town.

"How come you're stopping here?"

"To get you a tennis racquet."

"Gosh, Daddy, all they have here is little old cheap ones. Aren't we going to Dothan? I was hoping for a nice one, like the one you all gave Anne."

"I'm sorry, son, but right now your mother says we can't spend that kind of money. Let's get what we can afford, then later we'll see about a better one."

For the first time I realized that our family fortunes had fallen. He bought me the five-dollar Western Auto racquet, and I went out for and made the team, but it was one of the first true disappointments of my life. Suddenly the best was out of reach for us Walls.

Within a year of my starting to work in the hospital young Dr. McLeod left to set up practice in his hometown of Moultrie. If he gave Daddy a reason, Mother nor Anne nor I ever knew what it was. When no effort was made to replace him I worried about Daddy's having so much work to do. Mother, on the other hand, remarked that it saved paying an associate's salary. I satisfied myself with the thought that Daddy was holding that special spot for me. It might take a few years, but eventually we'd partner up. Doctor Wall and Little Doc, just as I'd always dreamed.

DURING THOSE BUSY YEARS while Daddy's attention to essentials ebbed, calls for his help still poured in. When somebody knocked at our side door at 10:00 p.m. one October Saturday, I opened the door to a gruesome sight. First I thought some pal in blackface was playing a Halloween prank, his chin drooping to his chest and what looked like fake blood streaming from both sides of his neck down his white shirt. When he spoke, though, I knew it was no prank. That blood was all too real, and the staggering colored man seemed unable to hold up his head.

"Uh, 'scuse me for bothering y'all," he said, "but I needs the doctor right bad."

"Daddy!" I hollered. "Come quick, there's a man here that needs you." I gaped at the gouts of blood all over our side-porch floor. "My gosh, what happened?"

He gave a little embarrassed laugh as I went on staring at the top of his bowed head.

"I been cut."

"My God, who did it?"

"Don't know. Couldn't halfway see."

Daddy had told me colored folks always said they didn't know who threw the lye in their face, or cut them, or set their house afire. They knew, but they were scared that if they told they'd get something worse the next time.

Behind me Daddy's big voice boomed out. "Great day, man, what happened?"

"Somebody done cut me. Please, Doctor sir, you got to help me." Clearly weak from loss of blood, the man clung to the door jamb to keep from collapsing.

Daddy said, "How'd you get here?"

"My brother, he brung me."

Daddy peered out into the night. "He still here?"

"No sir, he gone on."

"I'll get my bag and carry you to the hospital."

I wasn't going to let that man bleed all over Daddy's nice Chevrolet. "Wait, Daddy, let me find something to lay over the seat."

He studied me for a second, then said, "Get it quick and come on."

After I brought back an old quilt and spread it over the back seat, the three of us set off for the hospital, me up front with Daddy, the victim groaning in back. His head lolled so far down on his chest I thought a hard bump in the road might snap it loose.

At the hospital we helped him into the emergency room, and I watched closely as Daddy injected the local anesthetic with great delicacy, waited for it to take effect, then cleaned the wounds and took pains suturing the muscles around the back of the man's neck. After what seemed like hours he closed the skin, and to my amazement, the man raised his head.

"Doctor, I sure do thank you. How much I owe you?"

Daddy said, "Oh, I reckon eight dollars ought to be about right."

"Yes sir, well, I ain't got the money right now, but I'll pay you soon as I can."

I was indignant. He had gotten Daddy out at night, been driven to the hospital and stitched up, the whole thing taking a couple of hours, yet he had known the entire time that he couldn't pay. It didn't seem to bother Daddy. All in a night's work.

Medicine would never be a boring profession, I saw that clearly, and I was all the more determined to become a doctor—with one difference. I was going to get paid.

ONE SATURDAY when Daddy didn't need me at the hospital, my pal Charles and I decided to take in a picture show. I asked Mother for the necessary quarter, but she said, "I don't have any money in the house at the moment. Don't you know the combination to your daddy's safe?"

I nodded, for he trusted me that much. Even Mother didn't know it.

"Go look in there," she said. "I think he has some money in it."

Then I remembered. He'd shown us a paper sack full of nickels and told us a country woman had brought that sack of coins when she came in to have her baby. Daddy said she'd saved up those nickels two or three at a time, week by week, till she had enough to pay his twenty-five dollar fee, and for some reason he kept those nickels in his safe.

I didn't think he'd mind my taking a little money—he never stinted where our entertainment was concerned. I went to his closet, turned the combination on the safe, helped myself to a handful of nickels—buffalo nickels, mostly—closed the safe, and set the sack on a closet shelf for future use.

For quite a while thereafter I never lacked spending money. Ice cream, Cokes, movies, comic books, bicycle tires—whatever the need, I had the wherewithal. But a couple of years later I heard Daddy ask Mother, "Hallie, do you know what became of that paper sack of nickels in my safe?"

I spoke up. "I know, Daddy. A long time ago Charles and I were going to the picture show, and I needed a quarter to get in. Mother didn't have any money to give me, and you weren't here, so she told me to go get what I needed."

His impressive bulk seemed to loom even larger as I watched. Usually with me he was even-tempered and generous to a fault, but he'd let you know in a hurry if you stepped over the line. My confession did not sit well with him at all. I could see the shock and disappointment on his face and began to regret having said a word.

Finally he said, "You helped yourself to that sack full of coins?"

"Yes, sir, I did."

He was breathing hard, his face mottled. "Where's the money now?"

"I spent it."

His eyes stayed fixed on mine. "Spent it for what?"

"Ice cream, candy, funnybooks, whatever I wanted. I didn't think you'd mind. You always give me money when I ask."

"Sit down, son."

I sat down. At least he hadn't told me to turn around and bend over.

"Do you know where those nickels came from?"

"Yes, sir, a patient saved them up to pay for delivering her baby."

"That's right, five hundred nickels. That's twenty-five dollars, isn't it?"

"Yes sir, it sure is. How come you didn't put the money in the bank?"

He gazed at me for a long time before he answered. "It wasn't the twenty-five dollars that mattered, son. I kept that sack of nickels to remind me of that woman's sacrifice."

PHYSICIANS AND SURGEONS are supposed to hold in confidence whatever happens in their practices, but any doctor's family knows that some experiences inevitably leak out. If the doctor's spouse and children are smart, they keep quiet about what they know. While I wasn't particularly wise, I had sense enough to respect confidences Daddy shared with me, because I knew he was fostering my interest in medicine.

We were headed for the oyster bar after a baseball game when he said, "Some folks came in from Colquitt today, and you'll never guess what was wrong with their little girl."

"No, what?"

"One of the local charlatans—I won't mention names—had already seen her and told those parents she needed her appendix out that same day."

"And did she?"

His laughter made his big belly shake. He'd made very little headway at losing that hundred pounds. "She did not. Her stomach was all blown up, and she was crying, she was hurting so bad. But she didn't have a bit more appendicitis than you. If they'd let that man open her abdomen he'd have killed her."

"What did you do?"

"First I talked to the family. At MCG, you know, Doctor Sydenstricker always told us, 'Gentlemen, if you talk to your patients long enough, they'll tell you what's wrong with them.' I asked what she'd eaten lately, and right off the bat the mama told me she'd brought home two or three pounds of extra-nice grapes from the store.

"I know how children will do, of course, and I kept questioning till I found out this child had gotten into those grapes and eaten every one. It was a great treat, you see."

"Did that give her appendicitis?"

"What it gave her was an almighty impaction in her bowel. After I won her trust, she let me examine her. First I felt her belly for a mass, then explored with a finger in her rectum and felt this stony obstruction. By then she had calmed down, and I pared a wooden tongue blade down to reasonable size and gently used it to break up that mass."

My stomach hurt just hearing about it.

He flashed me a grin. "I had a pretty good idea what it was. A mass about like concrete blocked that child's bowel, and I knew it had to come out. So I dug and dug with that tongue blade, and when that thing finally split"—he let out another of his great contagious laughs—"why, son, you never saw so many grape seeds in your life!"

"Whew!" My stomach felt better. "I bet she was glad you could help her."

"She was, and her parents were even gladder when I told them if that obstruction hadn't come out she'd have got gangrene of the bowel and died. I'm sure my competitor resented losing the case to me, but

that's one appendectomy he was lucky to miss, if he'd had the sense to
know it."

ONE OF OUR RARE FAMILY vacations took place at Highlands, North
Carolina, in the summer of 1950. Daddy got in touch with a realtor and
rented a cabin for us. In addition to Mother, Anne, and me, an employee
of Daddy's named Herman Bailey was hired to cook for us and also drive,
as Mother refused to drive in the mountains and Anne didn't yet have
a license. It was a wonderful trip. Daddy took us to see "Unto These
Hills" in Cherokee, and along with the rest of us Herman enjoyed the
sight-seeing and choosing gifts to carry home to his family.

Once we got back home, Daddy approached the Rotary Club with
the idea of bringing a similar historical drama to the Kolomoki Mounds
as a tourist attraction for our area, only to be told he was crazy. His vision
and ideas were just too big for Blakely.

Throughout those four years while Daddy was out of politics, his
interest in it never waned. In the wake of the three-governors debacle
Governor Thompson had done a more than decent job. Then, in 1948,
a special election put Herman Talmadge in office, this time as the legiti-
mate governor.

Standing on the sidelines was too much for Daddy. He wanted to
get back into the fray. Despite the demands of his practice and other
obligations, progress through politics exercised that old allure. Herman
Talmadge was not just treading in his father's footsteps. People saw that
he had newer, better ideas about state government, and Daddy wanted
to be there to exercise what influence he could.

So in 1950 when Early County's turn for the Ninth District seat
came around, he offered himself as a candidate. Mother was dead set
against it, knowing what his absence would cost. By then the hospital
had a big staff: five nurses, three practical nurses, two orderlies, and two
cooks. It was an extremely busy place. Later even more help would be
added: several nurses' aides, recent high school graduates who aspired
to do hospital work.

"You can't do it, Henry," she said. "This time you wouldn't just be leaving a practice to languish. You'd be leaving a hospital that's running in the red, and those monthly payments due on your loan. That's sixty thousand dollars you owe the RFC."

He didn't respond.

"And then there's that delinquent income tax. Henry, you can't do it."

Daddy ignored her. He was a take-charge man, and Mother couldn't tell him what he could or couldn't do. At least on this round the periodontal ordeal was behind him, and with insulin his diabetes was under better control. None of that cut any ice with her. Headstrong, that's what he was. Daddy simply turned a deaf ear and won himself another two-year term.

BEFORE HE LEFT FOR ATLANTA we had all noticed a change in him. No longer so vibrant or energetic, now he was late most everywhere and could never be depended on to show up for special family events. Mother constantly had to remind him where he needed to be. Never noted for his punctuality, now he let time just dissolve away. At home he would close the door to his room and stay there for the longest time, or sit on the side of his bed and stare into space. Poor man, I thought, he had so much on his mind.

At Mother's urging, Daddy's loyal friend Dick Dismuke decided a "rest cure" was what Daddy needed, so he and another friend, Capt. Jack Dominey, drove Daddy out to Hot Springs, Arkansas. Whatever the purpose may have been, it failed. Daddy had a wonderful time as he always did on trips with his male friends, but he didn't change his ways. For Mother he brought back a diamond ring for which he'd paid $400 at an auction; she refused it, saying they had far too much debt for her to wear such a thing.

FINDING ENOUGH qualified help was always a challenge in our small town, and when an R.N. named Jane Howell applied for the job of head nurse, Daddy hired her. She came from previous employment by a doctor in nearby Edison, and it didn't bother Daddy that her father-in-law was his old nemesis, Sheriff Howell. He figured anybody deserved a chance. Once hired, Mrs. Howell urged Daddy to employ a colored practical nurse she'd worked with before, and Daddy also hired Willie Mae King.

Though he expected to be away for most of the next few months, he made no move to hire a business manager and, more important, never looked closely into the background of either new employee. Focused on going back to the senate, he had no qualms about going off to Atlanta leaving a new R.N. in charge.

That spring Anne graduated from high school with highest honors and a medal for academic excellence—but great disappointment over Daddy's absence from the event. He vowed that he had come in late and taken a seat in the back, but Anne swore she never saw him there. The diamond ring Mother had rejected became her graduation gift, and that autumn she went away to Georgia State College for Women in Milledgeville—not her first choice, but there wasn't money for going out of state.

What was happening? We'd had an idyllic childhood. Now everything was turning sour. At fourteen, still working in the hospital after

Senator Wall and fellow senator, 1951.

school and weekends, I was quickly forced to grow up before my time. Daddy was away one night when I found Willie Mae passed out at her desk. She didn't look sick, nor could I catch any whiff of alcohol. I'd seen enough drugged patients in the hospital to recognize the signs, and I was suspicious. When I shook her and asked what was wrong, she barely roused. That night I stayed extra-late in the hospital to make sure nothing went wrong.

I told Mother about it the next day, then told Daddy as soon as he came home. Nothing was done. Not even reprimanded, Willie Mae stayed on.

Along about that same time Daddy, needing more capable help, hired a quite intelligent and pleasant young high school graduate named Juanita Turner. Eager to learn everything she could, Juanita proved to be a quick study who caught on to things the first time Daddy explained them to her. An understanding soon grew between them that was almost like a kindly uncle and admiring niece.

Meanwhile, Mrs. Howell—Jane—was ordering all the supplies and medications. I knew that, because all the deliveries came to the hospital: items from hospital suppliers, medications from local drugstores. Medications required prescription, so obviously Jane Howell was sending out prescriptions. I figured that was her job. She checked in the orders and kept the inventories, and I often saw her and her practical-nurse pal whispering and laughing together when they worked the same shift. At times one or the other would stop by the hospital even when it wasn't her regular shift.

Something did not feel right. I couldn't put my finger on it—just a gut feeling that something fishy was going on.

AT HOME one of my regular chores was collecting our household trash to burn in the backyard. Shortly after Daddy's time in Atlanta ended and he was back home, I had found some small, rubber-topped, glass vials in the trash burner. Never having come across such things in our trash, I picked up one to examine it and made out a series of numbers on the label, along with the word "Demerol."

Demerol was a narcotic, I knew that. Those vials had held injectable drugs. I was scared. At the hospital Mrs. Howell kept narcotics under lock and key, and the local pharmacists maintained records of such items. I built the fire up to a light blaze, dropped the vials back in, and made sure the labels burned to ashes. Why didn't I mention my discovery to Daddy? Some possibilities are just too frightening to entertain.

I ached to forget my worries and get on with normal teenage life. I had no trouble amusing myself after Daddy managed to buy me two wonderful gifts—a Harley-Davidson 125 and my own twenty-gauge L. C. Smith double-barreled shotgun. It was a good thing I enjoyed them so much, for they were the last lavish presents I would have.

A crack shot himself, Daddy had instructed me early on in handling guns. He had a fine collection of firearms and had won many a turkey at Thanksgiving and Christmas shoots sponsored by local clubs. As "insurance" for his travels in the countryside on dark nights, he always carried a loaded pistol in the glove box of his car, and he'd taught me to shoot that as well as a rifle at pop-bottle targets. On our first quail-hunting trip he'd rejoiced with me when I bagged a bird with my first shot. We'd always had great fun going to carnivals and county fairs together, where he racked up prize after shooting-gallery prize until the carnie running the booth ordered him, invariably, to move on.

Boys in South Georgia grew up steeped in the outdoor life. Now that I had my own shotgun I went bird-hunting any time I could find two or three others to help cover the field. When I wasn't hunting, I buzzed all over town on that Harley. And as soon as baseball season came around, I went out for the team.

We never had much family time with Daddy unless we went on a trip somewhere, away from the demands of his practice and politics, and such outings weren't always delightful. Things between my parents grew more and more tense, and Mother could say or do embarrassing things—like the time in a dimly lit, nightclub sort of restaurant in Florida, when she insisted that Daddy bring a flashlight from the car so she could read the menu. Many times he'd excuse himself to go to the men's room and stay for an unusually long time, coming back less nervy, more relaxed. Anne would roll her eyes, but I kept my mouth shut.

It came as a terrific shock to me in 1952 when I walked up our driveway from school past an unfamiliar black-and-white Ford Victoria and learned that Daddy had traded in our family's two cars for this one. For years Mother had had one and he'd had another. But now money was even tighter. Our family fortunes had definitely slipped.

Even so, when summer came we planned to return to Highlands. It was to be the last such family holiday, and unfortunately it ended on a very sour note. Herman had moved north to take a civil-service job, but Anne was old enough now to help with the driving. Jane Howell's hospital sidekick Willie Mae, having heard Herman's glowing reports, offered to take his place as cook and help with what little housekeeping there was. When Daddy agreed to take her, our course was set for disaster.

The Victoria was a sporty two-door model, and with three of us riding in the back seat—one being Willie Mae—we were hideously cramped. It was a long, long way to Highlands, and we had scarcely arrived at the cabin when Willie Mae went into withdrawal from whatever drugs she was on. It was horrible. Not only was she absolutely no help, it was all Daddy could do just to keep her alive. Finally we gave up on the vacation, piled into the car, and made the long trip back home with sick Willie Mae never uttering a word.

Thereafter Mother had no use whatever for Willie Mãe and insisted that Daddy fire her. "She's a liability in the hospital," Mother said, but he declared LPNs were too hard to find, and furthermore he didn't want to take food out of a family's mouth. He probably talked to Willie Mae about her problem and tried to get her to give up whatever she was on, but he was in no position to lecture her, and no doubt Willie Mae knew it.

BY THAT TIME I had resigned myself to doing without any more "extras," since all Daddy's "extra" money had gone for my gun and my Harley. I could still participate in school sports and thoroughly enjoyed them. That year I played football and baseball, and while we had learned not to depend on Daddy to be anyplace on time, he managed to make it to all my games. I attracted a sweet girlfriend named Daphner and started to

**W. H. Wall, M.D., with wife Hallie and children Anne
and Henry Jr., 1952.**

date. Life was still good, so long as I ignored the feeling I got around those two hospital nurses and didn't think about the burnt narcotic vials.

Our last family event that was at all festive had to do with Daddy's senate term—a stay in Atlanta at the Henry Grady and dinner at the Capital City Club, followed by a swank function at the Piedmont Driving Club. Where the money for the trip came from I have no idea, but Mother considered it important enough to bring Anne from Milledgeville to join us. While Daddy seemed a bit detached and somewhat lacking in judgment during the affairs, that was the last truly celebratory occasion we ever shared.

From my early teens I always had one or two summer jobs that provided welcome spending money, so I didn't have to ask Mother or Daddy for any. I wasn't particularly surprised when Mother took matters in hand and started giving piano lessons at our house, even though she had always been content to stay in the background and make a home for us, her only outside interests being her music, playing bridge, and civic organizations such as PTA.

She was already working at the hospital during the day, and it came as a real jolt for me when she began teaching piano in rural schools as well. None of my friends' mothers had outside jobs. Something was seriously wrong. The solid ground of our lives was shifting under my feet.

Wasn't Daddy at all concerned? Mother certainly was. If so, he didn't show it. He didn't even seem bothered when the utility company cut off power to the hospital for a delinquent account. Eager to help, I went out to the bamboo grove behind the hospital and cut a long, heavy pole, then carried it where the power line came in from the street. The linemen had separated the outside feeder line just a few inches from the connection point on the building. Foolhardy as only a teenage boy can be, I risked electrocution by using my pole to make contact between the outside line and the terminal. And the tremendous power surging through the wire held the connection fast.

I thought I was being resourceful. It didn't seem like stealing, though that's what it was—stealing electricity from the power company. Ominous forces quite as powerful as the energy coursing through that wire were gathering around us, and I lived and breathed in the daily apprehension that all was not well. It was more than a teenage boy was equipped to handle.

Chapter 5

I began to find more drug vials in the backyard burner, even in the trash inside the house. They could only come from one place—Daddy's medical bag, the one he always carried to and from the hospital and out on house calls. Why didn't he discard them at the hospital with empty containers from other drugs? There could be only one explanation. He was taking the narcotic himself and concealing the evidence. I was too scared to find out. I just cut the labels from the vials with my Barlow knife and tore them up. More dark clouds. I lived with daily dread that when those clouds broke, we would suffer a terrible storm.

Finally the awful day came. Mother wasn't in the hospital office at the time, but I was polishing the hall floor when the nurse responsible for putting patients in examining rooms came to me.

"Little Doc, stop a minute, please."

I held the machine steady and cut it off. "What is it?"

"The waiting room's really backed up, and I can't find your daddy."

"Isn't his car here?"

"Right there in the drive where he always parks."

I went looking, and when I didn't find him I thought of the private bathroom between his office and the emergency entrance. That bathroom door was locked. I knocked and called, knocked and called—so scared my heart raced. Was he in there, unconscious with a heart attack? After I tried knocking and calling again louder with no success, I went to his big mahogany desk, found his passkey, and came back to open the door. I might open that door to find him dead. Daddy wasn't the healthiest person around. Anything could happen.

When I got the door open, there he was, fully dressed except for his suit coat, sitting on the closed toilet but slumped unresponsive against the side wall. Something dreadful had happened. The picture popped into my mind of Willie Mae slumped over her desk—Daddy's attitude and behavior were exactly the same. Quickly I closed the door behind me and kept my voice low.

"Daddy! What's the matter?" I wouldn't shake him, afraid he might fall.

He seemed to struggle back from some far distant place—like a disoriented swimmer trying to surface from deep underwater.

"Huh?"

"Daddy, listen to me. The waiting room's overflowing with patients. You're supposed to be taking care of them."

On the shelf above the washbasin I spotted an empty syringe and another of those scary vials, half-full. I picked up the vial. "What's this?"

He rubbed his eyes, trying to pull himself together, then reached for it.

"No," I said. "Leave it alone." I dropped the vial into my pocket. I had seen everything, and he knew it.

"Sorry, son, I must have dozed off."

"Look, Daddy, I know what you're doing. I know you're taking something, because I've been finding these vials in the trash at home. You have to stop. You *have* to." Hot tears burned my eyes. "If you don't stop this, you'll ruin everything."

I had never once spoken critically to my father. It nearly killed me, but I had to do it.

"Believe me, I'm trying," he said, in the weariest voice in the world.

"I mean it. This is serious business. Trying's not enough. You *have to stop!*"

He'd obviously given himself an overdose. With wobbly hands and unfocused eyes, he made a feeble effort to arrange his clothes, then struggled to his feet and fumbled for the syringe.

"Let me go put this away."

"No." I folded my arms. "You're in no shape to see anybody, certainly not the nurses or the patients. I'll say you're sick and need to go home.

They can tell the patients to come back later. Leave everything here, I'll put it away."

When he stumbled as if he might fall, I took hold of his arm to guide him from the bathroom out to his car. He was groping at the driver's door when I walked him around the car.

"No, Daddy. You get in on this side and wait. I'll be back in a minute to drive you home." I went back inside to store the syringe and the vial out of sight, then came back to the car. I didn't yet have a driver's license, but rather than let him drive I decided to take a chance. He had let me drive plenty of times on empty country roads, and this was an emergency.

Back home Mother was giving a piano lesson, so I had to help him to his room. After I got off his shoes, his belt, and his coat, he lay back on his bed and dozed off. I waited in my own room for the last piano pupil to leave.

When I heard the front door close I went into the living room, Mother was gathering up some sheet music.

The only way was to say it straight out.

"Listen, Mother, I have some real bad news. I found Daddy passed out in the bathroom at the hospital. He'd injected himself with Demerol and overdosed."

She sank silently onto the piano bench and steadied herself. "I knew it was bound to happen. Lord help us." She bowed her head and closed her eyes.

"You knew? For God's sake, how?"

"Oh, son, he kept on taking that stuff long after his dental work was finished." Wearily, she shook her head. "Don't you know how he's been these last few years? I've dreaded something like this for ever so long."

Having hoped for consolation, I felt even more helpless. "Good grief, Mother! Why didn't you tell him he had to stop?"

"Oh, I did, time and again. Anne and I both talked to him, tried to get him to get help. Remember when Dick and Jack took him to Hot Springs? We hoped that would do the trick, but it didn't. You can't make him do anything unless he wants to. He says he needs it to work."

"But that's what all dope fiends say. They all say they need it!"

She seemed to cave in on herself as I watched. "He has to work, son. You know how much is at stake."

"Work, heck! Think what'll happen if anybody finds out. Why, he'll lose his license, no telling what. I bet it's against the law, what he's doing. If no doctor's prescribing it, he has to be taking it from the hospital. Where else would he get it?"

At that she stood up, still steadying herself against the piano. "You're not telling me anything new. Addicted doctors can be convicted of crimes. It's the worst secret in the world. All we can do is hide it and pray he'll quit."

"But there has to be something more we can do!"

"I don't know of one thing."

I realized how long it had been since I'd seen my mother smile. She said, "Can you imagine the scandal if it came out that a member of the state medical board was a drug addict? There's nothing else for it. We have to keep it quiet."

When she turned away, sat back down, and began to play the Mills Brothers favorite "You Always Hurt the One You Love," I knew further discussion was useless. She always found it easier to lose herself in playing the piano or "resting" for hours in bed than coming to grips with painful, ugly realities. I understand now that Mother was chronically depressed. In her situation, who wouldn't have been?

That day marked the beginning of what felt like a permanent hundred-pound pack on my back. I couldn't keep such a threatening secret forever. It was enough to make anybody crack, not to mention a teenage kid. Daddy did his best thereafter to conceal his habit, but for Mother and me the cat was out of the bag. While the patient flow continued to fall off, he spent more and more hours at the hospital. I couldn't deny what I knew. My daddy was a dope fiend, and everything in our world was at stake.

IN THE MONTHS THAT FOLLOWED just two things brought any lightness to my life, and even those gave only temporary relief. As soon as I got my driver's license, whenever I could use our one car my girlfriend Daphner and I dated steadily. She was fun to be with, attractive, and very smart. I dreamed of marrying her and taking her to live in a town a thousand miles away, where nobody knew us and nothing bad could happen. That pretty picture would have to wait for college and medical school. Of course I couldn't tell her what I knew. I just did my best to carry on as usual, put on a smiling front, and act as if everything were fine. It was the hardest work I ever did.

The only other relief was anything that made me laugh. Amazingly, Daddy was still the source, many a time. His sense of humor was intact, and I was old enough to appreciate it fully. So did plenty of others in town, as I found out when I went in the barbershop to get my fashionable flattop trimmed.

The barber flung out the sheet and tied it around my neck. "Heard about your Daddy and Teddy T," he said. I knew who he meant, because that was the local nickname for our town's fattest man. Teddy was so huge he'd had to modify his car before he could get behind the steering wheel. The wags claimed Teddy hadn't seen a thing below his belt in years.

"You heard more than me," I said.

The regular loungers grinned. "Shucks, Little Doc," one said, "I thought everybody in town knowed it. It ain't no secret. Why, Teddy goes around telling it on hisself."

I said, "Then I reckon you'll have to tell me."

The storyteller reared back in his chair and cleared his throat. "What it was, y'see, old Teddy come in complaining to Doc that his belly was hurting him awful bad. Doc asked what he'd ate, and Teddy said, 'Oh, about the same as usual.' But that didn't satisfy Doc. He kept dogging Teddy, wanting to know every mouthful he'd ate. Finally Teddy said, 'I did go over to Dothan last night, and I had me a right nice dinner while I was there.' Doc said for him to go on and tell what it was.

"Teddy told him, 'Well, let's see. I had me a chicken, fried, and a nice T-bone steak after that, and a passel of fried taters and onions, 'bout eight ears of corn, ten or 'leven biscuits, I reckon, and best part of a apple pie.'"

I felt my eyes bugging out. "Good grief. What did Daddy do?"

"Told him to drop his pants and bend over. With that belly of his Teddy couldn't hardly bend over, but he done the best he could."

"Then what happened?"

"Doc took his time a-looking over Teddy's hindparts—and God knows they's enough of 'em. Then he said in this real serious voice like a preacher, y'know how Doc'll do, he says to Teddy, 'I've found your problem.' Teddy whips his head around. 'Tell me quick, Doc. How bad is it?' And Doc says, 'You've only got one asshole.'"

Oh, man. Did laughing ever feel good.

DURING DADDY'S SECOND SENATE TERM, for all his secret worries and ours, he was able to accomplish more good things for Georgia. He'd served on nine important committees, the Committee for Public Health being the one he cared about most. Governor Herman Talmadge, elected to a four-year term in the same year Daddy was re-elected, turned out to be a capable administrator and far better governor than most people expected.

Among Governor Talmadge's goals was increasing the number of qualified physicians in the state. Daddy and Dr. Lombard Kelley from the Medical College had seen the same need and told the legislature MCG could graduate twenty-five more physicians each year, provided a new 400-bed teaching hospital could be built in Augusta. But in that earlier term, money for the project had not been approved.

Now, with the governor's support, Daddy asked the legislature again to allocate the necessary funds. He played a vital role in bringing the project to fruition, pushed through approval of state funding for a third of the cost, and secured a Hill-Burton grant for the rest. At last MCG could build its new hospital. From the well of the Georgia Senate, Cobb County's Otis Brumby proposed naming it for Daddy in honor of his leadership, but in the end it was christened Eugene Talmadge Memorial Hospital, probably as a sort of tribute to his son. The old Wild Man from Sugar Creek got the honors, though he'd had nothing to do with the project.

MY FEARS INCREASED greatly while Daddy remained in the senate. I knew a lot more about his business, at a time when our house of cards began to tremble for sure. The Internal Revenue Service filed liens for unpaid taxes on every piece of Daddy's property and ordered him to sell the hospital to cover the debt. Sell the hospital, the dream he had waited so long to realize? Unthinkable. To this day I don't know how he managed it, but Daddy came up with the money. For the time being he hung on, yet in my gut I knew the whole shebang was about to fall apart.

Toward the end of that year a curious distraction came along. Daddy was in Atlanta on state business and I was working at the hospital when a crew from the town's sanitation department pulled up in front, unloaded their equipment, and cranked up a jackhammer to dig up the street. I went out to see what was going on.

"Hey, can you all keep it quiet? This is a hospital, we can't have a lot of noise." We had no patients in Daddy's absence, but I didn't tell them that.

The foreman motioned the jackhammer man to cut it off. He took off his cap, then spat a big gob of tobacco juice.

"Can't help it, Little Doc, we got orders straight from the mayor. They sent us out here to check on the hospital sewer, say it ain't never been hooked up to the main."

"Come on. We've never had any sewer problems, and this hospital's been here five years."

"I can't help it. That's what the man said. Claims it ain't never been hooked up to the sewer at all. We got orders to fix it."

The whole thing seemed mighty odd to me. If the hospital sewer wasn't hooked up, what had happened to five years' worth of sewage? We'd have seen backed-up toilets, signs of leakage, standing water. We hadn't seen a thing.

And what did the mayor have to do with it, anyway? Mack Strickland, Daddy's former well-wisher, was no longer Blakely's mayor. Now the incumbent was Dr. Jack Standifer, my daddy's competitor, who spent more time being a Shriner than he did tending the sick.

I'd looked into the hall once that led from the back of Fryer's Drugstore to Dr. Standifer's office, and once was enough. The place gave me the creeps.

Chairs for the few patients lined the dim hallway, and on shelves over the chairs big demijohns displayed disgusting specimens, like a two-headed calf—definitely not the kind of thing to make sick folks perk up. The contrast with Daddy's modern, bright, beautifully equipped examining rooms was striking. And now Dr. Standifer was Blakely's mayor. I wondered whether he wore that fez in the mayor's office.

The jackhammer roared to life again, but I held up my hand. "Can't you all hold on a minute? Not connected—are you sure that's what they said?"

"Now, Little Doc, you listen real good, 'cause this is the last time I aim to tell you. My orders is to dig up the hospital drain, get it hooked up to the sewer good and tight." He nodded to the jackhammer man. "Go on. We got work to do." Get lost, kid, that's what he was saying.

When I went inside and told the nurses what the man had said, Willie Mae said, "They don't know what they talking about." For once the dopey woman had a point.

"Hush," Mrs. Howell said, "and get back to work." She seemed mighty busy all of a sudden, going through old patient charts. "We've got too much to do here to worry about any sewer."

With Daddy away and no patients in the hospital I couldn't see how she had a thing to do. I noticed her filling out a prescription pad. Why was she ordering medications, and how, without Daddy there to sign?

Daddy's sensible assistant Juanita was as puzzled about the sewer as me. "I can't understand it. I've been here quite a while, and we've never had trouble with any drain. Do you suppose Dr. Wall knows about this?"

"Juanita, I'm stumped. He wouldn't have let a thing like that slip by."

Her rising laugh made me feel better. "You're telling the truth now. He knows everything about this hospital, down to the last pair of scissors, last brick in the walls."

"Well, he's sure going to know about this as soon as I can tell him."

At home Mother said it was the first she'd heard of any such oversight.

"Should I have stopped them from digging it up?"

"You couldn't. The street and the sewer system belong to the town, they don't belong to the hospital. If the sanitation department sent out a crew, they're supposed to do as they're told. Maybe the foreman misunderstood."

"No ma'am, he was real emphatic about it. Not connected to the sewer, that's what he told me, twice. Oh, and the other thing he said—the mayor told the sanitation department to send them out."

Mother frowned. "The mayor? Doctor Standifer's the mayor now."

Yes, Dr. Standifer certainly was the mayor. Why was he taking such an interest in Wall Hospital all of a sudden, when he hadn't bothered to attend the grand opening or admit a single patient even after Daddy invited him to?

By the time Daddy came home from Atlanta the crew had finished its work and repaved Columbia Street. I told him about it anyway.

"So, what do you think?"

He shrugged. "I don't know. The sewer connection was definitely made. Maybe there was a leak, maybe the connection failed. Whatever it was, they must have fixed it."

We never gave it another thought.

A bright spot appeared that fall on the local political scene with the election of a new sheriff—Mr. C. C. "Tuck" Swann. Down at the barbershop after Sheriff Swann's victory, somebody said, "Ain't it a pity, them poor fellers in jail won't have no more bootleg whiskey to drink," and everyone laughed. Sid Howell had recently been the butt of the joke when he discovered all his "private stock" missing; one of the inmates had fashioned a siphon and drawn off every drop.

Sheriff Howell may have ensured his own defeat, in fact, after he hired an ex–highway patrolman to sit in his personal car on the highway outside Blakely and issue speeding tickets to Florida-bound tourists and unlucky locals. Didn't matter how fast they were—or weren't—traveling, it was either pay in cash or come back later to contest the ticket in court. Disgruntled drivers paid up, and Sid Howell took his cut. When enough folks got tired of it, they voted him out.

So Daddy's old antagonist was finally out of office and out of power. He could do his worst to smear Daddy's name, but too many knew Howell's dirty ways to re-elect him. The colored citizens of Blakely in particular rejoiced. Good riddance to bad rubbish was what I thought. As I grew older I'd lost my fear of the man, because I towered over him and could have pinned the scrawny old crook at the first fall.

With all Daddy's reserves gone to pay the IRS, when the November payment on his RFC loan fell due he let that slide. Neither Mother nor I knew of the lapse, only that he was neglecting many things. Other people noticed. The stream of patients that had grown so large over the years, then diminished somewhat, now fell off dramatically.

Daddy's drug dependency had assumed such a central role in his life that he moved in a dreamlike world, truly believing all his problems would work out. It was a fantasy, a castle in the clouds. Like every other addict, he disregarded reality when it stared him in the face. He still acted on the assumption that he could manage everything, for he always had.

THAT SAME FATEFUL NOVEMBER in 1952 a secret investigation began that would have the most far-reaching consequences of all. Keeping secrets in Blakely was difficult, but this one was closely guarded for months. Daddy didn't know, Mother didn't know, neither Anne nor I knew. Acting on a complaint, an agent from the U.S. Drug Enforcement Agency came to town to collect information from local pharmacies about narcotics prescriptions Daddy supposedly had signed. Somebody had blown a whistle, somebody with a grudge, somebody in a position of power. Maybe even a number of somebodies. Dr. Standifer? Jane or Sid Howell? All three of them?

No member of our family had any inkling of these behind-the-scenes maneuvers, but it wouldn't have mattered had we known. The damage was done.

In the meantime, Daddy's final senate term ended. Back to Blakely he came, but his addiction had made such inroads on his thinking and his ability to function that recouping his losses was impossible. Mother worked like a galley slave trying to bring the hospital accounts into the black, coming home to give piano lessons into the evening hours. Football practice kept me busy afternoons, and I went on working at the hospital evenings and weekends, though not getting paid.

Whenever I found a few hours to spend with Daphner I pushed my troubles to the back of my mind and tried to relax. It didn't work. Those dates were over far too quickly, and as soon as I took her home all the worries came flooding back. Mother needed me, and Daddy needed us both to guard his secret. We had the first of many unjoyful Christmases that year.

In the first week of February both Jane Howell and her sidekick quit their hospital jobs. As we were soon to learn, it would have been a fine thing had neither of them ever been hired. Jane's father-in-law must have learned about the DEA investigation and tipped her off, so that she in turn tipped off Willie Mae. Sid Howell also had to have known that the two women had ample cause to worry. Both were addicts, and Jane Howell was having Daddy sign blank prescriptions, then filling in the specifics herself—or, as all of us suspected, even forging his signature. When Anne told me later that she'd actually seen Jane sign Daddy's name to a prescription, we believed it was something she was supposed to do. There was so much we didn't know, and all of it would come back to haunt us.

Today, as an oral surgeon who deals daily with pain relief, and knowing what a fine physician Daddy was, I find it hard to imagine his being so heedless, even though I recognize how profoundly drug-dependent people's warped thinking affects their judgment.

While I worked at the hospital, Jane Howell certainly sent the drugstores many prescriptions to be filled, because I saw them delivered to the hospital. I didn't check to see what drugs she ordered, since Daddy had entrusted her with the job. Storing narcotics safely under lock and key and keeping an inventory of them were her responsibilities. Even after her employment ended, she came in to the hospital now and then, for as late as April her name appeared as an assistant in the surgical log.

Where was Daddy getting the drugs he took? My guess is that he ordered Demerol for patients who needed it, administered the appropriate portion, then kept the rest to use himself. Perhaps he was so far gone as to order narcotics in the names of others for his own use, though I don't like to believe it even today.

So AFTER FEBRUARY Juanita remained as Daddy's sole medical assistant. Mother had recognized Juanita's capabilities and paid for her to have further nursing training. It was too bad Daddy's thinking had become so haphazard, for otherwise he could have supplied documentation for Juanita to become a licensed practical nurse, as she was certainly qualified by training and experience. Another oversight among the multitude piling up.

In the months and years to come, Juanita's intelligence, integrity, and kindness would prove unparalleled blessings. I still count her as one of my family's most special friends. She cared about Daddy and always did what she could to help him, and in a fatherly way he cared about her. Her loyalty was unwavering, especially years later when she saw him so beleaguered and so ill.

Early that year Anne transferred from her in-state college to enter the University of Alabama where she pledged Chi Omega sorority, allowing her to live at the Chi Omega house. She was happier than we'd seen her in a long while. That spring she attracted a new beau, a popular Blakely fellow named Elvin Williams, known to his friends as "Jiggs." They soon were dating steadily, over Mother's objections. Jiggs had come up the hard way, and Mother wanted Anne to marry some young man of position who would inherit wealth. What mattered to me was that Anne was happy.

But once again she complained that her college bills were overdue, or that the university business office was dunning her about bounced checks. "It's humiliating," she wrote home. "Can't you all keep this from happening?" Apparently not; the problem was chronic.

In March the RFC gave Daddy one month to bring his loan payments up to date—if he failed, foreclosure would follow. Over a six-year period he had paid off twelve thousand dollars of the original loan, but the RFC wanted all its money and wanted it fast. Daddy didn't have forty-eight thousand dollars, and while he tried to arrange for other financing he failed to find a lender who would help. The local bankers must have known he was in dire straits.

I had no idea what we would do. The power company cut off power to the hospital once and for all, even taking down the outside wires. No effort with a bamboo pole would meet the need this time. Yet Daddy still believed he was in control. Some time before he'd bought a 4-HP gasoline generator but never had it installed. Now he called Charles Rice's dad to come and set it up, giving him enough power for the main rooms. He insisted that the neon sign out front be powered as well, so people would see it and know he was still open for business. All too late. Word was out. Doctor Wall and his fine brick hospital on Columbia Street were nearly finished.

He tried to carry on practicing as if everything were normal. Mother knew it wasn't, and so did I. We just waited for the axe to fall. In April Daddy performed his last hospital operation. It was obvious the establishment was on the verge of folding. Patients no longer poured in, and Daddy scrambled for money to keep going. He fought the collapse with everything he had, but it wasn't enough—his resources were tapped out. His competitors must have licked their chops, waiting for him to lose his fine facility so one or the other could snatch it up.

People talked. Outsiders had to know. That spring Daddy had what was termed a mild heart attack, and Anne came home briefly to see him after he was hospitalized at Phoebe Putney Hospital in Albany. There, as I recall, he was under the care of Dr. J. B. Redfearn, a cardiologist, because in doing research for this book I found a moving letter he wrote Daddy in April.

The letter's tone is that of a gentleman, a Christian, and a true physician:

Dear Doctor Wall:

Knowing a brother physician needs help urges me to speak frankly with the hope that you will understand that my only purpose is to help you.

You have one life to live and one license to practice medicine in Georgia. You cannot afford to sacrifice either. You have the reputation of a good citizen and a splendid physician, as well as an unusual ability in making friends. Beyond this you have a loving and adoring family that depends on you. Those precious children must not be let down.

No doubt you are too close up to see the picture clearly as a whole. Back up and look and decide. It may be possible to salvage part of your belongings or it may not. Save part of it if you can, but if you cannot, then save the body and invite the true man that you normally are to take over and then we can help you rebuild for a still more useful life housed in a body of normal weight guided by a contented mind. The body shows some crippling but it can be used as a noble dwelling place while you go about doing good. Maybe it might be better to start again elsewhere, but this you can do to the joy of your loved ones, your many friends, and to the great satisfaction of your Creator.

Take a few months where you can get a grip on yourself and rebuild, physically, mentally, and spiritually, and success will surely follow. It means more to that boy and girl of yours than it does to Mrs. Wall and you.

Sincerely yours,

J. A. Redfearn, M.D.

While this fine man didn't spell out in so many words his awareness that Daddy was addicted to drugs, it was obvious he knew. He was imploring Daddy to reach out for help while there was time. But reach out where, or to what? In 1953 there were no effective drug rehabilitation programs, no impaired-physicians committee ready to help. Doctor Redfearn simply saw Daddy on the road to ruin and hoped the right words from a caring friend might halt the self-destruction train. As for the Blakely doctors, not a one expressed any word of sympathy or offered help. Although Daddy could see no way to act on his friend's advice, the letter undoubtedly meant a great deal to him, because he kept it the rest of his life.

In May the RFC acted, filing a complaint for judgment against Daddy in Federal court. The hospital was lost. What more would we lose?

I got a job digging a sewage ditch at the new Kolomoki State Park, earning the grand total of $28.75 per week. The job was a killer. We were fifteen feet down in a ditch, shoveling dirt onto a platform above us so laborers higher up could shovel it all the way out. It was dangerous work. That ditch could cave in and crush us to death, so I was relieved when the foreman handed me a mop and a bucket of creosote and told me to climb up to treat the shake-shingle roof of a new building. Before I finished, my skin was so blistered I had to keep myself coated with thirty-weight motor oil. Soon I was so sick I had to quit the job.

Nevertheless, I held on to every dollar I'd made. There was no telling who might need it or when. Daddy and I got out to a baseball game whenever we could, and we still ate oysters afterward at Charlie's place. We were just putting one foot in front of the other. Our hearts weren't in any of it.

After the first summer-school session Anne did come home, only to be told there wasn't the money to send her back for the second. Undeterred, she got busy making herself some new fall clothes and set her sights on fall semester, planning to be back at Chi Omega early so she could help get ready for Rush.

She was already back in Tuscaloosa when the trap sprang. Late one August afternoon Daddy called to us as soon as he walked in the door.

"Hallie, son, you'd better come in here and sit down."

I had just finished cleaning up after another miserable day on the job, and Mother was lying down in her room before supper.

When I walked in the living room I noticed how pale and sweaty he looked.

"What is it, Daddy?"

"It's all over." His voice broke.

Mother had already sat down and clenched her hands in her lap.

"Oh, Henry, what's happened?"

"A U.S. marshal came to the hospital today and arrested me. Jane and Willie Mae were arrested too. We had to go to Camilla before we could make bond."

"My God, Daddy, arrested for what?" I don't know why I even asked, because I knew what it would be.

"Charged with conspiracy to violate the Harrison Act," Daddy said. "Obtaining narcotics by means of fictitious prescriptions. Same charges against all three."

Mother said, "Why didn't you call us?"

"I didn't want to worry you more than I had to. They let me call our friend Red Felder, he came straight down and went on my bond."

The picture of those two nurses whispering and laughing came back clearer than ever.

"The nurses," I said. "Are they in jail?"

"Oh, no," Daddy said. "Jane Howell's father-in-law, our fine ex-sheriff, came down and made bond for her."

"Good God. Willie Mae, what about her?"

To my amazement a flicker of a smile passed over Daddy's face. "That's real interesting. When Sid Howell bailed out Jane he brought along that son of his she's married to, and young Howell went on Willie Mae's bond."

I couldn't believe it. "Let me get this straight. You're telling us Sid Howell's son got that colored dope fiend out of jail?"

He nodded. "Makes you wonder, doesn't it?"

Throughout this exchange Mother had sat weeping quietly. Now I was also crying, and so was Daddy. I'd never known such a hopeless feeling. I went over to sit beside him.

"Daddy, what will we do?"

"Lick it," he said, but there was no conviction in his voice.

Mother wiped her eyes. "Henry, didn't you know about the nurses?"

"I don't want to talk about it any more," he said.

Why not? I'd long sensed that something bad was going on between those two. Hadn't Daddy seen it? Was he too preoccupied, or couldn't he bear to know?

That night the last words spoken came from Mother: "How in the world will we get out of this mess?"

Chapter 6

Daddy astonished us the next day by sending for Dr. Price Holland. Until then the only doctor in Blakely he had been on speaking terms with was Dr. Baxley. Why hadn't Daddy called him? I didn't understand. Nevertheless, Dr. Holland came, and Daddy asked him for a final shot of Demerol to ease him into the inevitable withdrawal. It must have cost him a great deal to ask such a thing of the man.

Jealous or not, at that point Dr. Holland must have felt compassion for Daddy, faced with the loss of his reputation, his livelihood, his hospital, everything that had fulfilled his purpose in life. To his credit Dr. Holland gave Daddy that final injection, and for days afterward Daddy endured the cravings without acting on them. I don't believe the misery of withdrawal was as long or as bad as he'd feared. If he'd known he could get clean without an agony of suffering he might have broken free sooner, and our lives would have taken a far different turn.

Anne had to be told what had happened. Mother called her at the Chi Omega house after dinner, forgetting that Alabama was an hour behind us. Anne had been at dinner, and after getting the news that Daddy had been indicted she was too upset to return to the table. When her roommate found her in their room crying, Anne told her what had happened and begged her not to reveal the family's shame.

Within a couple of weeks of Daddy's arrest a very strange thing had happened, and later that same month it happened again. Twice that August someone broke into Wall Hospital, *taking only the records relating to narcotics.* I knew that all doctors were required to keep records of drugs bought, drug inventories, and drugs dispensed to patients. Who would want Daddy's narcotics records, and why? And who would know where to find them without turning the whole place upside down? I could only think of four or five people, Jane Howell and her father-in-law topping the list. Sheriff Swann investigated, though no culprit was ever found. By this time so many bad things were happening that the burglaries and stolen records seemed minor by comparison.

Two months of waiting for the trial tested everyone's nerves. Daddy kept to his former routines as best he could, with the added necessity of consultations with his three attorneys. Two, Grady Rawls and Frank Twitty, Sr., were former colleagues from the Georgia legislature, both practicing in nearby towns. The third, Lowry Stone, Sr., was a Blakely man. Between the necessary conferences Daddy continued to see patients right up to the time of the trial. He'd been required to surrender his narcotics license, but that limitation made very little difference in his day-to-day practice now that he had no more surgical patients to attend.

With the threat of personal ruin hanging over his head, I can't conceive of the effort it must have cost him to meet his patients as usual, walk Blakely's streets, and do his best to greet people in his same cheerful way. He was a remarkably courageous man.

Mother had to return to her teaching job, and that too had to be a mortification to her soul. I went back to high school for my junior year—pure misery from the first hour.

We lived in a town of four thousand souls, and everybody was talking about us. Our Early County paper reported Daddy's and the nurses' arrests and the charges against them, as did the *Albany Herald*, read over much of South Georgia. I could hardly bear it when Daphner acted as if she barely knew me, and none of my other friends had any idea what to do or say. They avoided me or, if contact was unavoidable, managed not to notice me sleepwalking through the halls and classrooms. Every moment of every day seemed unendurable. I couldn't talk about our troubles with anybody. I didn't want to. Because my mind was in such turmoil that I couldn't take in what was being taught or remember it when asked to give it back, my grades took a nosedive.

I know now that when stress activates the primitive part of our brains, pushing us to "fight or flight," our ability to reason and remember drops dramatically. Too sad to fight, all I could think of was ways I might flee. Hurt and bewildered and far from grown-up, I saw how poorly I was doing in school, yet I couldn't help myself.

The one person with a kind word for me was Mr. Steve Summerhill, who coached our football team. He may not have been the world's greatest coach, but he was one of the world's kindest men. In a quiet moment he called me aside.

"Little Doc, you'll get through this," he said with a pat on my back. "It seems awful, but you'll make it. Keep your chin up, just keep moving ahead. I want you to know I'm thinking about you." After fifty years that good man's words still bring tears to my eyes.

As for Mother, she wore her bitterness like a neck brace. She'd always been a rather private person; now she was aloof. One lone friend out of all those we knew in Blakely came around to try to encourage her—Mrs. J. B. Rice, my friend Charles's mother. Neither our new minister at the Methodist Church, Mr. McKibben, nor any fellow church member came nor expressed concern. Certainly none of the other doctors' wives did. What misery Mother experienced at her teaching job I don't know, but those two months were a period of purgatory for us all. If anybody was spared it was Anne, living elsewhere and not faced with the daily pain. Even so, she had her own trials, because her tuition and sorority bills were always in arrears.

Anne confided her troubles to just one of her Blakely friends, the same one who'd recommended her for Chi Omega.

"Now, Anne," she said, "you're just as good as everybody else, and you mustn't let this tear you down." This good friend's encouragement helped Anne to get through the humiliations, although the hurt and its aftermath would extort a terrible toll. For years, whenever Daddy's name was mentioned, Anne burst into tears. In fact, thirty years would pass and much counseling would have to be undergone before she'd at last be able to sort it all out.

If the RFC followed through on its stated plan, the hospital would soon be foreclosed on and sold at auction. Daddy couldn't bear the thought. He began running an advertisement in the Atlanta papers: "South Georgia Tourist Motel For Sale." Five years before, in a move typical of his earlier farsightedness and systematic planning, he'd asked the hospital architect to arrange things so that if ever the building were no longer needed as a hospital, it could be converted to a motel. A few responses to the ads came in; nothing was settled.

As the days passed and the fog of Daddy's extended drug use began to clear, he became fully able to face the harsh reality of how much he and all of us stood to lose. At stake were his fine reputation in state politics, his medical practice, the hospital he'd invested in so heavily and been so proud of, the nurses' residence next door, in fact everything he owned— even our debt-free home on Flowers Drive. We stood to lose it all.

We moved through those endless days as through a death in the family with the corpse still lying in the house. It was worse even than a funeral, for in the wake of death friends and neighbors would have come bringing casseroles and flower arrangements, pitching in to help. None of it would have taken away the grief, but the kindness would have made a world of difference. We got no casseroles, no flowers, no help. The despair never let up.

LATE IN SEPTEMBER Daddy observed his fifty-first birthday. Monday, October 5, 1953, was the date set for the trial. A few days before it began, Mother was reading the latest issue of *Ladies Home Journal* and I was trying to make sense of a tough geometry problem when Daddy came into the living room.

"Hallie," he said, "I'd like you and Henry to come with me to my room."

Close to solving my problem, I didn't want to give up. "What for, Daddy? Can't it wait?"

"I want us to pray together," he said.

Mother and I exchanged surprised glances. She, Anne, and I attended church regularly, Daddy almost never. An earnest believer, he did his best to live a Christian life, but he was generally too busy making house calls or seeing patients to join us at church. With the exception of saying grace at meals, we did not pray together at home.

"Yes," Daddy said, "come with me, please. We have a terrible experience ahead of us, and this is the best preparation we can make."

When we saw how important it was to him, Mother laid her magazine aside and I put down my pencil and followed them to his room.

"Good," he said. "Now I want us all to kneel down together beside the bed."

We were all three in tears by the time Daddy started to pray aloud. I had never heard him do such a thing, and my heart stirred within me to hear that strong voice address the Creator in such a full and fervent way. I knelt there tasting salt at the corners of my lips, tears streaming from my closed eyes.

"Almighty Father," he said, "we ask your blessings tonight upon this troubled family. As the head of this household I come confessing my every shortcoming—as a husband, a father, as a physician, and as a Christian. I acknowledge my every weakness, and they are manifold. I know I have failed my profession, I have failed my family, and not one soul bears any responsibility for this situation but myself."

He never hesitated for a word, never faltered for a moment. "As you look upon our family gathered in prayer tonight before our coming ordeal, we ask your forgiveness for all our shortcomings and beseech your loving guidance and unfailing wisdom in the days ahead. We trust in your almighty power to sustain us and pray that you will ever lead us forward in strength and in constant faith. These things we ask in Jesus' blessed name, Amen."

Those few minutes in Daddy's room as we heard his confession and joined our aching hearts to his marked one of the two great spiritual experiences of my life. The other one would come all too soon.

DADDY SAID he didn't want me going to Albany for the start of the trial; he wanted me where I belonged, in school. Mother went, and so did Juanita, though the authorities never allowed Daddy's trusted helper inside the courtroom. Through three days of the trial that dear friend waited in the hallway, sitting on the floor for much of the time, and by the fourth day she was too ill with pneumonia to go back. I know Juanita's tender heart could scarcely have borne the sorrow of that fourth and final day.

Those first three nights back at home Daddy and Mother told me what had taken place. On the advice of his lawyers, Daddy entered a plea of not guilty, while the two nurses entered guilty pleas, having agreed to give evidence for the prosecution. We could only hope the lawyers were giving Daddy good advice. It was a jury trial, and I'd heard lawyers say how unpredictable juries are. Those nurses might be sworn to tell the truth, but we knew from sad experience that they could not be trusted.

On the trial's first day the DEA investigator testified that he was first called to Blakely to look into a large number of prescriptions purportedly signed by Daddy.

"Who would have sent for him?" I asked.

Daddy said, "I don't know, maybe one of the local pharmacists. Word has it that one of those fellows from Fryer's left on vacation right suddenly last week."

The DEA man said he'd been asked to return a second time after the chief of police reported a find of several hundred narcotics containers in the hospital drain.

"In the hospital drain? How would anybody know where to look?"

"Oh, there's a way," Daddy said. "Suddenly it's all crystal clear. Remember when the sanitation department sent a crew out to dig up the street? Somehow Dr. Standifer—excuse me, *Mayor* Standifer—got wind of something fishy going on at the hospital, and rather than coming to discuss it with me, he went behind my back and ordered a wire cage placed on that drain. Someone at the hospital was throwing away those vials, and that's how they were found."

"So somebody set you up. Do you know who it was?"

"Not yet," Daddy said. "But I'm plenty suspicious."

I folded my arms. "I never did believe that drain wasn't connected. It didn't make sense." It was entrapment, pure and simple.

During a three-month period, the DEA man also claimed, Wall Hospital *reported* use of more than ten thousand doses of narcotics. Anybody who was paying attention would have raised his eyebrows at a figure like that. During the period in question Mrs. Howell was the head nurse, and so far no one was making the point that Daddy relied on her to complete those required reports.

The DEA man also testified that Daddy, when questioned previously, had admitted to using "eighteen to twenty-five cc of Demerol over the past eighteen months for several ailments." Daddy's attorney Mr. Rawls objected, declaring that Daddy was questioned without being informed of his constitutional rights.

The judge's gavel came down: "Objection overruled." As one after another defense objection was overruled, Daddy's lawyer Mr. Stone complained that in more than forty years of practicing law, this was his first experience of a trial where lawyers were never allowed to object.

The more I heard, the more certain I felt that Daddy was being railroaded. I couldn't say a word to relieve his misery. All I could think of were those other doctors in Blakely, too jealous to come to the opening of the town's first modern hospital or send their patients to it afterward, but not too honorable to help set him up. And then there was the gang of Talmadgeites at the courthouse—chief among them Sid Howell—who'd resented Daddy's progressive positions over the years.

Daddy gave his word of honor to Mother and me that he'd never dropped any vials in the hospital drain, and we believed him. Even in the late stages of his addiction, he was too intelligent to do such a stupid thing. I'd seen some of those labeled vials in our backyard burner. They could be accounted for, and he wasn't about to take the risk of having them found by anyone on the outside.

We couldn't deny his dependence on the "nonaddictive" drug Demerol—though Mother refused ever to describe him as an addict. She always rationalized, saying he needed the drug because of the heavy pressures he carried. Yet no one had ever accused him of mismanaging any case or mistreating any patient. He had never been charged with a traffic offense, and he'd gone on functioning reasonably well up to the last moment. In fact, he was a high-functioning addict whose addiction was finally catching up with him. On some level he must have been relieved when the truth came out. He must have prayed, like Mother and Anne and me, for someone to throw him a life preserver. Instead, he would be robbed of the last shred of his dignity.

On the trial's second day Jane Howell, described in the Albany paper as the government's "star witness," claimed she had become addicted to Dilaudid while in Daddy's employ, adding that she was "later cured in a Birmingham hospital." Never brought out in the trial was the reality that she was already an addict when she and Willie Mae worked in the doctor's office in Edison, before coming to work for Daddy.

She acknowledged that in Blakely she'd obtained drugs by having Daddy sign and give her blank prescriptions, then filling in the specifics herself. "But Dr. Wall knew what they were for," she claimed. She also said on the stand that Daddy himself was an addict. Later her practical-nurse follower took the stand and admitted being addicted to morphine as well as Dilaudid. I couldn't recall Daddy's ever prescribing Dilaudid for any patient. She said she got the drugs from Mrs. Howell but "couldn't remember" whether she had taken narcotics before coming to work for Daddy. She too claimed she had been "cured."

The third day's testimony began with Dr. Dismuke, Daddy's room-mate, who'd been a pharmacist before he entered medical school. He spoke about his own thirty-bed hospital in Ocilla and specified what quantities of narcotics he ordered for use there. If Daddy was an addict, Dr. Dismuke said, he had never seen any sign of it. He recalled Daddy's recent week-long hospitalization in Albany and stated he would be "quite surprised" if someone using narcotics in the amounts being attributed to Daddy could get through an abstinent week. Anybody in that situation "would have to have an awful strong constitution," Dr. Dismuke said. However fine his intentions, it didn't sound to me as if his testimony did Daddy much good. In days to come he would make up for it a thousand times over, however, with concrete help that made a world of difference to our family.

That third day two prominent Blakely citizens also spoke on Daddy's behalf—Sheriff Swann, and D. C. "Babe" Morgan, who'd gone with Sid Howell and Daddy to call on Annie and Dumah. Both testified to Daddy's outstanding reputation in the community, and Sheriff Swann referred, but only in passing, to the two August burglaries at the hospital and the disappearance of narcotics records from the place.

One of Daddy's attorneys pointed out that of the twenty-some prescriptions named in the indictment, *only five* were entirely in Daddy's own handwriting. The rest were in another hand, presumably that of Jane Howell. No handwriting expert was brought in—another misstep on the part of Daddy's legal team, though one of them did state that Daddy had "never had any trouble" until after Mrs. Howell came to work for him.

At noon on the third day, Daddy himself was finally called to the stand. He acknowledged that while he had been "careless" in leaving signed prescription blanks for Mrs. Howell to fill in, he—like many physicians—had entrusted her with that responsibility because she was a professional, a registered nurse, just as he had trusted her to keep the required records.

There it was again—those crucial records, the ones that had disappeared in the burglaries two months before. Who had taken them and why? Who had anticipated any reason why they shouldn't be found? During the trial those questions were never posed.

Daddy also testified that when he hired Mrs. Howell and Willie Mae he didn't know they were addicts but began to be suspicious of both shortly before they quit—about the time the DEA investigation began. Was their departure coincidental? Unlikely, we thought.

On Thursday, October 8, I stayed away from school in order to drive to Albany with my parents for the conclusion of the trial and sentencing. It was the most miserable feeling in the world, facing the flight of stairs that led to those courtroom doors. We felt certain that when court adjourned we would have to walk out without Daddy.

Heartsick, I lagged behind as Daddy ushered Mother up the stairs and inside, and as I hesitated, a Marine sergeant came out of his recruiting office and approached me as if to speak. I didn't know the man. Was he coming over to invite me to sign up? I longed so painfully for escape that if I'd been eighteen I might have gone.

No, it wasn't that. He knew who I was, and he drew me into a sort of alcove there at the foot of the stairs.

"Son, I know this seems like the worst thing in the world," he said—a virtual echo of Coach Summerhill's words.

I ducked my head, not knowing what to say.

"Sure, I know," he said, "right now it's awful, but you'll get through it."

As he gave my shoulder an encouraging pat my eyes filled with unshed tears.

"You just keep that chin up. You'll make it, you'll be fine. One day you'll look back on this and feel proud of the way you handled it."

"Yes, sir." I swallowed hard. "Thanks."

The prestigious Marine uniform, the colorful decorations arrayed on his chest, no doubt for combat in Korea—his words, which made me feel that I *could* get through this terrible time in our lives . . . I never knew his name, but I never forgot his kindness.

Pride was a word to hang on to. I was proud of how Daddy was handling his humiliation. Maybe one day I could do half as well.

"ALL BE UPSTANDING," the bailiff ordered inside the courtroom, and we rose as the judge entered and took his seat. "Oyez, oyez, oyez," the bailiff proclaimed, "this court is now in session. The Honorable T. Hoyt Davis presiding." From that point it didn't take long for matters to reach a conclusion. Their guilty pleas had bought the two nurses punishment of some sort, yet I was stunned to hear the judge sentence each one to eighteen months' *probation*—no time in prison at all. Both had admitted guilt, and Jane Howell had dragged her sidekick into the mess and gone on to compound Daddy's shortcomings by forging prescriptions. Eighteen months' probation was barely a slap on the wrist.

Then Daddy's turn came. He and his attorneys stood up to hear the sentence, Daddy bracing himself against the table's edge. Judge Davis said the jury had found Daddy guilty—at that word, Daddy flinched as if he'd been struck, and Mother gasped while I covered my face with my hands.

"Guilty," the judge said, "on four out of the twenty counts listed in the conspiracy indictment, on the basis of fictitious prescriptions"—*allegedly* fictitious, I wanted to shout—"written for just two patients." Two! If that were a crime, God knows it was crime on a minuscule scale.

When I heard him add that he believed Daddy was an addict who couldn't "stand on his own" and needed "treatment," my dashed hopes revived a tiny bit. He meant to send Daddy somewhere to get help. That was all any of us wanted, help for Daddy.

At that moment, if things weren't already bad enough, Mother suffered an additional humiliation. She was going through a miserable change of life and in the midst of the proceedings had to get up suddenly in front of everybody and hurry out of the courtroom to take care of a menopausal crisis. She must have wanted to die. I wanted to drop through the floor.

The judge went on to tell Daddy that whatever the sentence might be, "it wouldn't be so much punishment." Still on his feet, Daddy listened, steadying himself against the attorneys' table. Judge Davis said he hoped Daddy could be sent to some institution where he could be "cured and straightened out"—exactly what Mother and I had prayed for. Maybe the outlook wasn't all bad. Maybe it wouldn't be prison, maybe some hospital like the one in Birmingham where Jane Howell claimed she'd been "cured."

It was not to be. Mother was back in the courtroom in time to hear the judge sentence Daddy to eighteen months—but the anticipated word didn't come. Not eighteen months' probation, eighteen months *in Federal prison.*

Daddy's shoulders sagged, his face turned ashen. I couldn't catch my breath. Mother clutched my hand hard enough to break bones. And then we had to watch as two bailiffs came over to lead Daddy out of our sight by the courtroom's back door. The sickening finality swept over me. Daddy had lost, he was gone. It was over.

We were still reeling from this blow when Daddy's lawyers tried to make us feel better by sharing knowledge they had. "It will probably be a Federal prison hospital for addicts in Lexington, Kentucky," they said. Well, at least it was called a hospital—people got treatment in hospitals. We tried to console ourselves with that crumb. I still wasn't sure my legs would hold me when I tried to stand up. As for Daddy, he looked seventy years old.

"Now, Mrs. Wall," Daddy's Blakely lawyer said, "I don't want you worrying about the doctor. We intend to file an appeal right away."

Mother just looked at him. "And you think that will help?"

"We have to try," he said.

"No, we can't carry it any further." Her eyes seemed utterly dead. "The money's all gone."

They told us Daddy had been taken away to the Brooks County jail in Quitman. Drained of all emotion, Mother and I had to drive back to Blakely with everything our family had worked for in ruins. I'd never felt so disheartened or exhausted. Mother must have felt even worse, because now the burden of everything would fall on her, and she wasn't used to much responsibility beyond keeping house and bringing up children.

"I'll carry you to see him, Mother," I promised, "just as soon as you can go. This Saturday, maybe we can go then. Don't worry, now. Daddy will tell you what to do."

She just went on staring straight ahead.

Scattered family members were waiting anxiously to hear the outcome of the trial. It was no good holding back, for the papers whose front pages were carrying the trial on a day-by-day basis would report the final result tomorrow. Anne had to be told, and Daddy's relatives in Ellaville and elsewhere. Everyone offered sympathy. None of it helped. My daddy was in jail, convicted of a felony, on his way to Federal prison. I didn't know when I'd see him again or how; in the meantime, we had to survive. That was the most pressing issue of all.

While he was still in Quitman Anne came home and went down there with Mother once to see him; I didn't go, because I had to be in school. Soon Daddy was transferred closer to home, to the Mitchell County jail in Camilla, and I went with Mother to see him there. It was awful to walk into that county jail and see the kind of people Daddy was locked up with. He was a sick man, yet there he was. I could barely believe it was happening.

Less than a year before, he'd had the freedom of Governor Herman Talmadge's office. Former governors were his close friends, Georgia's secretary of state one of the closest. The Atlanta papers had often quoted Daddy with approval and praised his forward-thinking initiatives. He'd been the moving force in bringing a new teaching hospital to our state, had spear-headed vital change for the mental-health community, had helped to establish county health departments statewide, had been a respected member of the Georgia Board of Medical Examiners.

Now here he was in drab jail clothes, shuffling in backless slippers like all the other inmates. And yet his words were optimistic.

"I don't want you all worrying about me," he told us. "I'll be all right. I'll only be here a little while, and where they're sending me after that—it's a prison *hospital*—I'm sure I'll be helped." Off the drugs for more than a month, he was coming back to his old self. Heartening, even inspiring, to me.

But Mother said, "Really, Henry, we'll never hold up our heads in Blakely again."

"We have to, Mother," I said. "That's all there is to it. I'll do everything possible to help till Daddy gets home."

"Shucks," Daddy said, "you all don't worry any more about Blakely. Fred Hand came to see me, you know, Speaker of the Georgia House, and these doctors in Camilla have been wonderful. It's the difference in night and day from what we've known at home. One after another they've come to see me, made sure I get my insulin, encouraged me every way they can. It would do your heart good to see them. They're still shaking their heads in disbelief."

Daddy's report was a breakthrough for me. We'd all been so caught up in Blakely's poisonous jealousies that we'd lost sight of his undiminished stature on the statewide scene. Here were colleagues coming to see him, demonstrating their support. They had brought Daddy out of his spiritual abasement, and seeing that was more than enough to lift my spirits.

Mother grimaced as if she hadn't heard. "So, how long do you suppose it will be? The full eighteen months?"

"No, no more than three. The lawyers tell me most of the people in Lexington stay about that long. I may not make it home for Christmas, but you can bet I'll be back by the New Year."

"Then tell me this," Mother said. "In the meantime, just how are we supposed to live?"

"Why, Mother," I said, "you have your salary, and your piano pupils, and I plan to do everything I can—"

"The motel ad," Daddy said. "We've already had at least a dozen inquiries. Now, Hallie, I want you to go ahead and sell the building as a hospital or a motel, either way, the minute somebody makes you a reasonable offer. After that you'll have plenty to live on till I get back."

The consummate optimist couldn't consider the possibility that everything might not work out, for until now everything always had. He'd told me once of driving to New Orleans with several Blakely friends including Guy Maddox, the peanut-butter man, to see the Georgia Bulldogs play in the Sugar Bowl. The quartet had neglected to make reservations, and all the hotels in New Orleans and even in nearby towns were booked up for the big game. They tried five different hotels, with Mr. Maddox going in to see about rooms. "Sorry, no vacancies," he was told every time. Apparently his peanut money didn't carry any weight in Gulfport, Mississippi, or anywhere in Louisiana.

Then Daddy took charge. "Let's go back to that first hotel, the best one. And this time I'll go in."

Whoever was driving did as he said, and his fellow travelers waited for him outside the hotel, mystified when he came back within a few minutes waving the key to a top-floor suite.

"Come on," he said, "you fellows unload your bags."

Mr. Maddox said, "Henry, how in the hell did you do that?"

In that carrying voice all his friends knew so well, he said, "I just walked up to the front desk and said 'Senator Wall's here to check in.' The desk clerk looked real worried, and he said, 'Senator, we don't have your reservation.' So then I said, 'Do you mean to tell me my secretary messed this thing up, after I've driven here all the way from Georgia?'

Daddy knew that hotels always kept some rooms back for special guests. And sure enough, in a little bit the manager came out to say they'd had a last-minute cancellation for a suite on the top floor. Not just a room, a top-floor suite. So he and his friends lived the life of Riley during their stay. That was a typical example of the way Daddy could make things happen.

Now, though, selling the hospital as a motel sounded like a mighty long shot. I couldn't believe any potential buyer would see a motel. Motel guests arrived in cars, and the hospital had parking space for just a few. Anybody with good sense would recognize the huge amount of expense such a conversion would take.

"Come on, Daddy. What about beds? Motel guests aren't going to sleep in hospital beds."

"Why, of course they won't!" he said. "I expect to sell the hospital equipment separately. We'll realize plenty of money from that to put in proper beds."

On the drive home Mother and I had almost nothing to say. For the next eighteen months Daddy was guaranteed room and board, such as it was. Whatever we had would be entirely up to us.

TWO DAYS LATER, still swamped in sadness and shame, we saw posters go up all over town advertising the auction of all Daddy's property in one lot—the hospital, nurses' residence, even our home. So much for any motel.

How Mother felt I don't know. I felt paralyzed. I could see us out on the street with nothing, penniless, homeless. Who would pay our bills? A few piano lessons sure wasn't going to do it.

I got my first surprise from Mother when the finance company sent a man out to the house.

"I'm here to repossess your Ford," he told her.

She drew herself up straight. "Repossess it? Our only car? You most certainly will not," she told the startled repo man. "Young man, you just come back about this time tomorrow, and I'll have the money to take care of it."

After he left, I said, "My gosh, Mother, why'd you tell him that?"

"Because we have to have a car. That's all there is to it."

I still don't know where she got the money. This was a side of Mother I'd never seen—all her embarrassment, anger, and hurt submerged, to be replaced by iron resolve. That astonishing core nature would surface again and again.

Gossip always ran through Blakely like a dose of salts. I still had to go to high school five days a week, and in the hallway I passed my football teammate Carl Farris telling a huddle of classmates he planned "to play hookey to go to the Wall auction." I wanted to kill them all.

Mother said she was sure the other doctors would flock to the sale. "Your father says Dr. Holland's always wanted that hospital."

"Why don't you go talk to him, see if he'll buy it ahead of time?"

"I can't do that," she said. "Handing it over to one of these Blakely doctors would break your Daddy's heart."

Every night I had the world's worst time going to sleep. Being a teenager was awful in itself, and with everything that had happened I was so embarrassed I wanted to disappear. Long after midnight I'd lie awake trying to get up the courage to run away. But where could I go, with no money and no way to survive? Scarcely old enough to shave, I was suddenly the man of the house. I couldn't leave Mother to deal with the mess on her own. That would be dishonorable, and I couldn't dishonor my family.

My only escape on those late sorrowful nights was to Station WWL in New Orleans. I would lie in bed in the dark and listen to their late-night Dixieland jazz on my bedside radio, until that happy music eventually lulled me into a restless sleep.

Every morning I'd wake up worn out, with a weight like lead in my belly. It was autumn, yet all the color had drained out of the world. I never felt like eating breakfast, never knew how I'd make it through another school day. Coach Summerhill continued to let me know quietly that I had his support, but I didn't want anybody talking to me about it at all. I just wanted to crawl in a hole and be left alone.

About this time a visitor came to our house. I was mowing the lawn when a short, pleasant-looking man drove up in a Kaiser automobile, parked, walked up to the front door, and knocked. Mother let him in, so I kept mowing. After a few minutes she called me inside to the living room.

"Son, you probably know Mister D. M. Carter from the Church of Christ. He's come to offer his help. Mister Carter, this is Henry, Junior, my son."

When he stood I managed to shake his hand, hardly believing what I'd heard. Somebody in Blakely, offering help?

He smiled. "That's right, young man." We all sat back down. He had a good handshake and a kind face. "Your dad's been my family's doctor for years, as well as the doctor for my manufacturing plant. I think the world of Doctor Wall, and I know this is an awful time for you and your mother. I want to help you all with a little money."

Mother shook her head. "Son, I've already told Mr. Carter we can't accept his money. We appreciate the offer, but we'll make it one way or another."

"A loan, then," Mr. Carter said. "You and Dr. Wall can repay it after he gets back on his feet."

"Take it, Mother," I said. "You know we can use the help." I knew it went hard with her to accept what she saw as charity. "Think of all Daddy's done for this town and these people. Why not accept it? I'm sure Daddy would want you to. Don't worry, Mr. Carter, I'll help Mother pay you back."

"Good man," Mr. Carter said. "I can offer a little something else, too. I mentioned my plant—we manufacture peanut-shelling machines and grain elevators, and I'd like you to come to work for me."

Drop out of school? It was tempting, but Daddy wouldn't like that a bit. "I'm sorry, Mister Carter, but I'm still in high school. If the offer's still good next summer, I'd sure like to come then."

He got up and shook my hand again. "The job's yours whenever you can take it. Well, I'll be on my way." He reached to his inside coat pocket, drew out an envelope, and laid it on the lamp table on his way out.

After he was gone Mother and I opened it to find five $100 bills. "Well,

Mother," I said, "I guess there's one Christian man left in Blakely."

With such huge losses looming, Mother was doing everything she could think of to salvage the situation and wrote at least one letter to an out-of-town physician:

Dear Doctor S.,-

No doubt you have read of Dr. Wall's trial and that he is to go to Lexington, Kentucky for treatment. . . . [While] I will not have time to go into a lengthy letter, I will say that Dr. Wall was impressed with you and was in hopes that he could get cleared of the charges against him and that you could work out something together. . . . The purpose of this letter is to tell you that the hospital is to be sold in front of the courthouse doors on Wednesday, October 14. . . . I thought that you might be interested in coming down and bidding on it. It is my honest belief that the majority of the people in this town would be glad if a new Doctor and especially one with your qualifications would buy it and come here to practice. It will be a bargain at $75,000 and might be bid in for less than that. I could put you in touch with the right parties and believe it could be refinanced. . . . There will be some other bidders, but I would like to see you get it if possible.

Yours Sincerely,

Mrs. W. H. Wall

Dr. S. decided no.

Our immediate challenge was moving what we could out of the hospital. The auction flyers stated that the equipment would be sold with the hospital, but there were personal possessions of Daddy's we needed to salvage and store. Juanita and her husband Ernest came to our aid, as they would many more times. Ernest was just as admirable and good-hearted as Juanita, the son of a colored farmer unusual in that he wasn't a sharecropper but farmed his own land. Ernest and I moved what we could to our back porch, our barn, anywhere we could find room to store things. As we moved in more and more stuff, Mother and Juanita did their best to bring order to the conglomeration.

One thing we couldn't move because of its weight and size was Daddy's big mahogany desk. Leaving it behind would break his heart, but we couldn't help it. We did the best we could working at fever pitch. At every day's end I was more tired even than I'd been when I was digging that ditch out at Kolomoki Park. Ernest was used to hard work, but I could tell the effort took a lot out of him, too.

Waves of sadness kept washing over me. I'd never had to help clear a house after a death in the family. Now I knew how it must feel.

The night before the auction, Dr. Dismuke called. When I answered, he asked how I was holding up, and I mumbled that I was doing okay. Then he asked if Mother was there, so I called her to the phone and went back to my room to work on a book report. I could hear her say, "Why, hello, Dick . . . Yes, it surely has. . . .You are? . . . Oh, my. . . . I really don't know what to say. . . . Well, if that's what you want to do—"

After she hung up, she came to my room.

"He told me not to worry about things," she said. "He said he knows it's been a horrible time for us, but this auction's going to turn out better than I think. He's driving up tomorrow with Captain Dominey and Jack Willis, because the three of them mean to see that we're looked after. He said I should stop worrying, that they'd see us tomorrow."

"Gosh, Mother, what d'you suppose he means?"

Her eyebrows lifted, and she shrugged. "I don't know, but we'll never have a better friend than Dick. If he says he's going to help, he will. Whatever happens, I feel a little better. Now maybe tonight I can sleep."

I think both of us slept better that night than we had since the trial.

THE MOMENT had arrived. Six days after Daddy's sentencing. all his property went up for auction on Blakely's courthouse steps. We knew there would be a big crowd. Some would come out of curiosity, while others would come hoping to get a fine piece of property at a bargain.

The morning of the auction I set off for school like a condemned man. Somehow I got through the day, and even before I started home I heard all about it. Carl Farris and the other hookey-players were back to tell their classmates about it, and hearing their story made me feel like I'd been right there.

A few minutes before the auction was to start, Carl said, a big new Cadillac drove up to park in front of the courthouse, and three men got out and moved to the front ranks of the crowd. People started whispering: "Who's that? Anybody know who those three are?" Nobody did. The bidding began, and right away somebody bid twenty thousand dollars, then somebody else bid twenty-five, and somebody else bid thirty.

At that point all conversation stopped as people waited to see if the bid would go higher. Somebody said, "Reckon the Walls are ruined."

But then, Carl said, the man driving the Cadillac—a good-looking guy about six and a half feet tall, wearing rimless glasses, a suit and tie but no hat—called out: "Sixty thousand firm for the lot!"

Gasps ran through the crowd. "Did he say sixty thousand?" "Hell yes, he did." "Well, I never in my life!"

The auctioneer seized his opportunity. "Sixty thousand, I have a bid of sixty. Do I hear sixty-one?"

Nobody said a word.

"Sixty and a half?"

Still no further bids. People were just staring at each other in amazement.

The auctioneer raised his voice again. "Sixty thousand once, sixty thousand twice—" Nobody could believe what was happening. BANG! The gavel came down. "SOLD! Sold, for sixty thousand dollars to the tall gentleman wearing glasses in the front row!"

The mystery was absolute. Nobody knew the strangers or what they wanted with Dr. Wall's property. We weren't ruined, just a little shook up. A victory after so much heartbreak.

Once the commotion died down, Dick Dismuke and the other two men came by our house and sat down to work out the details. Dick said they would find a buyer who wanted the hospital for its original purpose and hold onto the nurses' residence for Daddy when he came back to town. As for our house on Flowers Drive, Mother and I could continue to live there without obligation until some more permanent arrangement could be made. In the long run, they meant for the deed to revert to Mother and wanted to fix it so she and Daddy could pay off the debt over time. I couldn't imagine how it would ever get paid, but Mother told them she was determined to pay off every dime.

After that Mother and I kept mum. She and I were the only ones in town who knew the strangers, or why they had done such an astonishing thing. Daddy's big-hearted friends had saved our family bacon. We'd escaped the buzzards of Blakely.

Chapter 7

Our troubles weren't over, only temporarily eased. But when we went to see Daddy in Camilla to report on the outcome of the auction, he was wearing a cheerful face.

"If I have to be in jail," he said, "thank God it's this one, and not Sid Howell's hell."

I said, "Sid Howell doesn't run it any more, Daddy. Did you forget about Mr. Swann?"

"Thank God for that, too," he said.

On our next visit other relatives joined us, for the weirdest family reunion imaginable. There we were with our kinfolk, united in body and spirit in the exercise yard at the Mitchell County jail. Most of the other prisoners were colored, and surrounded by so many colored families we Walls stuck out like marshmallows in a barrel of molasses. All the relatives there for this surreal visit chatted and commented on absent family members and matters of mutual interest, just as if we were in a perfectly normal setting on a perfectly normal day.

Daddy said, "There's just one thing missing from this reunion, that big old table loaded down with plenty of good home-cooked food." Little did we suspect that this would be the last family occasion with Daddy his normal self.

We couldn't understand the delay in sending him to Kentucky, and nobody would give us a reason for it. But finally the federal marshals came to transport him there. We got the details after they reached their destination. They had driven him, in handcuffs, from the southern to the northern boundary of Georgia, then put him up overnight in the jail at Chattanooga, Tennessee.

Next day they drove on to Kentucky, where he was incarcerated in the U.S. Public Health Service Hospital—a federal prison for drug offenders. His case number was M-35004-Lex. He was housed not in a cell but in a hospital-like room. On arrival he was examined by a physician and assured he would get his insulin on the appropriate schedule. For meals he went to a cafeteria, and he was told he'd be assigned work responsibilities around the building or on the grounds.

Like the other inmates, he was allowed one weekly phone call, and the first time he called he found something typically positive to say. He gave Mother the details of the trip from Camilla, then added, "You ought to see that jail in Chattanooga. It's the nicest one I was ever in. I tell you, Early County could take a leaf out of their book." When she told me that I wanted to cry. How could he take his plight so lightly?

Thereafter in his weekly calls and more frequent letters he tried to reassure us that he was all right and continued to instruct Mother on the handling of various business concerns. When she passed on the letters to me, I found his tone impatient—no doubt frustrated by his inability to help us. He couldn't realize how hard Mother was trying, or the lengths to which she went. She borrowed money on a life-insurance policy, and once that money was gone, she used up her entire inheritance of nine hundred dollars. She was arranging another life-insurance loan when Daddy ordered her to stop.

He signed his letters "Henry" or "Daddy" depending on the recipient, but under that signature always added either "William Henry Wall, M.D." or "W. H. Wall, M.D." Never had we known him to use the William of his name. Maybe it was a prison requirement; we took it as a signal that every letter was read before it left the prison.

DESPITE HER OWN heavy burden of cares, Mother knew how depressed and discouraged I felt. Having to go to school and try keep my spirits up was almost more than I could manage, and when I came in one afternoon she handed me my shotgun and said, "Why don't you go out and shoot some doves?"

I thought she was trying to cheer me up, reminding me of a favorite but neglected pastime. Anything was better than moping around at home, so I hunted up my shell vest and a box of shells, took my prized twenty-gauge, got on my Harley, and headed for my favorite dove field. When the pavement gave way to a dirt road, it was great fun whizzing along through thick honey-colored stands of broom's-edge. I flushed up a couple of coveys of quail along the way, and after passing the sedge fields noticed that most of the corn had been cut. That was good, it should bring the doves in. On a spur-of-the-moment outing I had little hope of bagging anything with nobody else fanned out to cover the dove field. It was just good to get away.

Once I got to the place and parked the Harley, I found good cover in a corner of the field and sat down. All the corn had been harvested, but plenty of nubbins and fallen kernels still lay on the ground. I sat there for a bit, thinking how good it felt to be out in the quiet, to smell the country smells, to feel the breeze on my face in a spot where in earlier days I'd had so much fun.

Straightaway the image of Daddy came to me, how he'd enjoyed teaching me to shoot and how good he was at it himself. If he were there he'd be giving me tips on the best way to go about it. I chambered my first two shells and waited. In the far distance somebody's coon hound yelped. From a nearby house I caught the fragrance of wood smoke, then a whiff of cooking collard greens. I expected a long wait before I saw any doves, maybe even none before dark.

Yet I had hardly settled down when, to my astonishment, fat doves began flocking into the field. When I stood up and took aim, knock-ing down two with my first shot, it marked the beginning of the most memorable hour of my life. I couldn't miss. Scores of birds seemed to launch themselves straight for the barrels of my gun, and I'd no more than knock down a couple when half a dozen more flew straight for the same spot. My heart pounded like crazy. I could hardly reload fast enough. If only I'd brought along enough shells I could have shot a hundred birds. I couldn't even take time to go out and collect the fallen doves, so many more were flying into range.

As I banged away, reloaded, banged away some more and still birds continued to fall, my excitement knew no bounds. I couldn't wait to go home and brag about what a good shot I was, how quickly I'd bagged so many birds. The wind just whistled through my close-cut hair as I bounced over that dirt road headed for home. Mother had been right, I felt so much better. Between her suggestion and the healing powers of Mother Nature, I felt like a youngster again instead of an old, tired man. Back on Flowers Drive I put up the Harley, then strode into the kitchen. The slam of the back door brought Mother from the front of the house.

"Any luck?"

I grinned and dropped my satchel on the kitchen table. "Look inside. I got my limit in less than an hour. Some kind of shooting, huh?"

"Good," Mother said. "After you pick and clean them we'll have them for supper."

She wasn't even smiling. "Gosh, Mother, I'm tired. I'd rather clean them after supper. We can have them tomorrow."

She sat down at the table and began to inspect the birds, then count them. "Until you clean them," she said, "there won't be any supper. I don't have a cent, and there's not another bite of food in this house."

I sank into a chair across from her. How could this be happening? No food in the house, no money at all? My daddy was a doctor, we lived in a nice house, my mother was a music teacher. I'd never known anybody who hadn't a thing to eat. Going out shooting and having such success had made me feel good for the first time in ages, but now waves of despair washed over me. I folded my arms on the tabletop and buried my face.

Not many minutes passed before I heard Mother's chair scrape across the floor. "Well, son—how long do you want us to wait?"

I raised my head to see her standing over the table, steely-eyed.

"Yes, ma'am, I'll have 'em cleaned real quick." I forgot about a shower and went out to get the job done, just glad I'd shot so many doves.

It was then that a mysterious certainty settled within me. The Almighty had chosen this means to put all my fears to rest. "I'll take care of you," was the message. "Don't worry. You'll always have enough."

It was the second profound spiritual experience of my life. *Thank you,* I said in my heart. *Dear Lord, thank you.*

Mother floured the doves and fried them in bacon drippings, and instead of gobbling them up hungrily as I usually did, this time I tried to make every morsel last. We had enough for supper and some left over for breakfast. And the next day, after two of Mother's pupils came bringing payment for their piano lessons, she was able to buy a few days' worth of food. From then on we might have grits and greens for supper, or some thin chicken soup, but we never had another day without some food in the house.

FROM ANNE'S REPORTS we knew that things were getting rather serious between her and Jiggs, and after Mother learned that Jiggs intended to go over to Tuscaloosa to see her, she asked him to come by the house. I figured she probably had something she wanted him to carry to Anne, but that wasn't it at all.

They sat down in our living room, Jiggs surely wondering what this was all about, when Mother blurted out, "Are you all thinking of going to Mississippi to get married?"

He looked flabbergasted. I knew he and Anne had talked a little about getting married at some point in the future, but they were far from even considering themselves engaged. "Uh . . . no, ma'am, Mrs. Wall. We weren't even thinking about such a thing."

"I just wanted to find out," Mother said. "But don't you think it might be a good idea?"

"Well, ma'am, you'd have to ask Anne about that."

Jiggs seemed both puzzled and embarrassed to be spoken to so bluntly, when he scarcely knew Mother other than to make polite conversation. Anne later told me that when he went on to Alabama and told her about the conversation, she was horrified. She couldn't figure out why Mother would say such a thing, since she claimed to disapprove of Jiggs as a suitor.

Jiggs speculated Mother was thinking that if they got married and he took over Anne's support, the family's financial burden would ease. He told Anne he loved her but wasn't about to rush into getting married, because he had every intention of seeing her go on to get her degree.

AROUND THANKSGIVING came the first really depressed-sounding letter from Daddy: "I will not be home this Xmas—nor probably next Xmas either, as I have no one to help me. I am really the 'goat' now. . . . If you intend to do anything, do it now and stop writing me to quit worrying and 'rest.' Silly thing . . . All I ask you is not to wait too long to wake up. . . . I was sent here to get me out of the way while the Vulchers [*sic*] made a clean sweep."

He seemed to believe it was still within Mother's power to sell the hospital as a motel, urging her to set a price of sixty-five thousand dollars on the building—or, if she could find someone who wanted it for a hospital, seventy-five thousand for building and equipment together. Why was he so confused? He'd been told that Dr. Dismuke and his friends had taken it on.

". . . . I have a new assignment of work. I am doing eight hours special nurse duty for an old black addict from Chicago that has advanced T.B. and gas gangrene infection of an arm. Of course he is in isolation." That didn't sound to us like any addiction treatment.

Mother began to think that Daddy's three-month prediction was unrealistic. She wrote letters to several people about it, including Daddy's lawyer Frank Twitty, who replied:

> . . . I had previously received a letter from Dr. Wall and had made overtures to Judge Davis, but very frankly I got very little encouragement from him. I have made other contacts to secure Dr. Wall's release but to be perfectly frank with you, it seems at this time that Dr. Wall is going to be forced to serve six months. I will continue my efforts, however, in his behalf.
>
> My very good friend, Mr. Adron Doran . . . former speaker of the house of representatives of Kentucky, was in Atlanta several days ago, and I told him about Dr. Wall, and I have just received a letter in which he stated that he and his wife had been out to see Dr. Wall and had a very pleasant visit and was going back and visit him often. I feel sure that this will be of great comfort to Dr. Wall while he is in Lexington.
>
> My suggestion is that we do everything possible to keep his spirits

up, and try to keep him from worrying. I feel that life will not by any means be over when he is released, but that he will be able to come home and earn a living for his family. You can expect my full cooperation.

While . . . during this season of the year you perhaps think that you do not have too much to be thankful for, maybe the new year of 1954 will bring new hope for a better life for you and the family, and you certainly have my prayer for this.

When we got a notice from prison authorities saying the only Christmas gifts "patients" could receive were money, hard candy, and shelled nuts, Mother decided that rather than send gifts, we would make a trip to see Daddy. She was already sending what little money she could to enable him to buy cigarettes, candy, toilet articles, etc. from the canteen.

So as soon as school let out for the Christmas holidays Mother, Anne, and I set off for Kentucky. It was a far from carefree journey. In one of the Tennessee towns along our way we had to wait while all traffic was stopped for a Christmas parade. The bands and marching groups included a contingent of Shriners, and when the lead convertible crept by carrying a familiar little figure in a red fez, we felt as if the imps of hell had pursued us. The "Grand Potentate" was Blakely's own Dr. Jack Standifer, one of the main persons responsible for our dreary trip.

I did the lion's share of the driving, and by the time we crossed the line from Tennessee into Kentucky we were dealing with significant snow. I had hardly ever seen the stuff, much less driven in such conditions, and had to learn by trial and error how to avoid sliding off the road. Between bouts of sadness for Daddy and regrets for having to spend my holiday in such a way, I would find myself marveling at the beautiful white-blanketed world, then lapse into guilt for enjoying it. By the time we checked into a motel on the outskirts of Lexington, we were pretty well worn out. Next morning we got in to see Daddy, and what a depressing business that was. Our visit had to be conducted at a table in the middle of a big room, with the three of us on one side and Daddy and an eagle-eyed prison official on the other. We were cautioned that no physical contact was allowed—no hugs, no handshakes, nothing. Even so, Daddy's pleasure at seeing us was plain. We did our best to say cheerful things, tell him how much we'd missed him, how glad we'd be when he came home. It was mighty hard to say those things without choking up.

We couldn't speak as freely as we'd have liked, though Daddy did talk about his responsibilities to the patient with advanced TB. Mother was terribly anxious that he might contract the illness, but he assured her every precaution was being taken.

Then she said, "What do they do to help you with your own problem?"

"Give me three meals a day and make sure I get my insulin."

She frowned. "Henry, we can do that at home while you go on working."

He shrugged. "It's out of our hands. Since we can't do anything about it, let's change the subject. One thing I've noticed here I don't like—some peculiar drug tests they're conducting on the inmates. I don't know what they're being given, but the ones that volunteer get rewarded in some way.

"It's really upsetting, because the ones who agree to take the stuff walk around like zombies or behave very strangely. Isbell's the doctor running it, and I don't mind telling you he rubs me the wrong way. I'll never know how any physician sworn to the Hippocratic Oath can treat his patients like that." But Isbell and his partners in crime, Doctors Winkler and Vogel, did exactly that when they followed instructions from the CIA to secretly experiment on unsuspecting patients at the Lexington "hospital." These experiments caused permanent damage to their brains.

This little piece of news really alarmed me. "You listen to me, Daddy," I said, "don't you dare volunteer for those tests!"

He laughed. "That's the last thing I'd do. I'm here to get better, not worse." He told us he missed us all every day, told Anne and me we looked well and said he was proud of us. It was a miserable visit, barely better than no visit at all. By the end of it he said again that he didn't expect to be home for a long time.

Mother said, "Frank Twitty thinks it won't be more than six months."

"We'll see," Daddy said.

BACK AT HOME Jiggs was very much in evidence, and before long Anne told us they were engaged. It was clear to me that Anne was very happy and that they loved each other. Mother said no more to them about Mississippi, but from something Daddy said later on in a letter, we knew she must have mentioned it to him.

Mother reacted in a very strange way to a phone call from Daddy on the first Sunday in January. I was getting used to her newfound strength in the face of adversity, but now as she listened she started to cry.

"Oh, Henry, what on earth are you talking about?"

From several feet away I could hear his voice booming but couldn't make out the words.

"Here, Mother." I reached for the phone. "Let me talk to him."

She handed it over, weeping. "Daddy, what is it?"

Daddy, who never panicked, sounded panicky. "Son, you all have to get me out of here right now! They've been giving me something, I don't know what it is, but it's made me crazier than a coot!"

"Hold on, Daddy. Did you sign up for those drug tests?"

"No! I promised I wouldn't. But they gave me something anyhow, in my food or drinks, some way or other. That skunk Isbell's behind it, I'm sure. I wouldn't trust the man behind a drop of rain.

"Now, son, listen to me. You all have to get me out of here as soon as you can! I'd rather be in the federal pen in Atlanta than in this hellhole!"

"My God, Daddy, you don't want to be in Atlanta. That's a terrible place! It—"

"Better than here," he said. "Tell your mother to write to Ellis, Herman Talmadge, Senator George, Senator Russell, anybody she can think of. If I stay here they'll kill me!"

"All right, Daddy, we will. What did you mean, they're trying to make you crazy?"

"Losing my mind, losing my grip on reality! Believe me, they've nearly done it. Tell Hallie, you all have to do everything you can to get me out of here. Call the judge! Don't wait!"

More composed, Mother took back the phone. "Henry, you must calm down—" then, "Oh, good heavens, no, Henry, not with your diabetes! You can't do that! It's far too dangerous for your health."

After another muffled blast she stopped arguing and began nodding. "All right. Yes, Henry, yes, I will. I understand. Yes, I give you my word. I'll do everything I can. Of course I'll ask Anne to help. All right. Now, take care of yourself. Yes. We will. Goodbye." She put down the receiver.

"What else did he say?"

"He's stopped eating in the cafeteria, quit drinking anything but tap water."

"My God, Mother, he can't do that! He's a diabetic, he'll—"

"*You* try telling him what he can't do, see how far you get."

"What will he do for food?"

She looked to the ceiling for a moment, then let out a long breath. "He told me to send him money to buy soup. Canned soup from the canteen, that's all he's eating, and not drinking a thing but water."

One more item for our gut-wrenching list of worries.

On the heels of that one came another. Mother called Anne in and told her there wasn't money enough to send her back to school.

"Oh, Mother—this year at Alabama was the very best year of my whole life! Can't we find the money somewhere?"

"There's nowhere to find it," Mother said.

Anne shouldn't have been surprised; she'd had to scrimp along from week to week ever since September.

"Well," she said, "what do you want me to do?"

Mother said, "Stay home, help Henry and me, get a job if you can find one."

Anne's shoulders sagged as she blew out a gigantic breath. "Good heavens, what job could I ever get in Blakely? I can't go to Atlanta, it would take everything I made just to live there."

"We'll have to think of something," Mother said. "Anyhow, I need help with all those letters your father wants written to get him home. I can't type, but you can."

Anne's head drooped, then she put a hand to her brow. "All right, I'll help. What else can I do?"

To distract herself, Anne walked downtown that afternoon and came back a couple of hours later with a small parcel of sewing notions. Sewing was one of her outlets, and she could remake some of her older clothes.

Jiggs was a welcome distraction from her disappointment at having to quit school. The two of them were certainly in love, and like me, Anne longed for a way out of our family mess. She dreaded going to Tuscaloosa to retrieve her clothes and other belongings, having already been humiliated when a sorority sister saw her reading a letter from Daddy and asked why it had words scissored out. Anne had to confess that her father's letters were censored because he was an inmate in a federal prison.

Daddy had always maintained our cars, and when Anne finally got ready to go to Tuscaloosa for her things none of us noticed how bald our Ford's tires were. My heart hurts for Anne right now just thinking about it, because between Blakely and Tuscaloosa she had *four* blowouts. How she came up with money to buy four recaps I don't know, but she did and recently reminded me, to my shame, that at the time I laid her out for not putting whitewall tires on our sporty car. I should have had more compassion, but teen-age boys are not noted for that quality.

Anne and Jiggs soon began to talk about marrying quite soon. When Anne told Mother, she did all she could to discourage it, and I followed her example.

"Anne," I said, "don't you want to wait till you finish your degree?"

"How can I? There's no money to send me, they won't give a doctor's daughter a scholarship, I can't find a job that pays anything, and Jiggs wants to marry and support me. What else do you suggest?"

"Wait," I said. "Just wait till Daddy comes home and things get better."

"No," she said. "I've had enough of this misery. If I can't be of any financial help here, I surely won't be a burden. We've set a date in April, after Daddy gets home. You know his lawyers say he'll only have to serve six months."

"Come on, Anne, a few months longer won't hurt. You might see it differently if you give it a little time."

She said, "You don't know a thing about it. I love Jiggs, and he loves me, and we're getting married in April. He's already asked his brother to come from Philadelphia to be his best man."

Though Mother and I kept trying to talk her out of the headlong rush, we never gained an inch. Daddy had to be told, and that would be hard. Mother wrote Daddy's new friend Mr. Doran asking him to tell Daddy and try to soften the blow. Jiggs—who was asking now to be called E. B.—very properly wrote him a letter, asking his consent for the marriage. Mother also asked Mr. Doran for any suggestions he might have about getting Daddy released after six months rather than eighteen. She told him how worried we were about his health, not to mention the economic hardships. He answered:

> . . . I know you must be deeply concerned over Ann[*sic*]'s sudden decision to drop out of school and get married. I visited Dr. Wall Saturday afternoon and found him in very good spirits except he, too, is quite disturbed over Ann's unwillingness to delay her marriage until she has finished her degree. . . . I am afraid he feels that his incarceration may have prompted Ann's sudden decision to drop out of school and get married thinking that she is a financial worry and burden to him. He did not say this to me but I think I read this between the lines though I do not wish that you say this to him. . . .
>
> I would suggest that you make an effort to see the judge and discuss with him the fact that consideration should be given to Dr. Wall's parole at the end of the six-months period. It may be that those who are advising against your seeing the judge [probably Frank Twitty] may be interested in seeing that Dr. Wall remains in the institution for the full length of his term.

Mother had never accepted the hard fact of Daddy's addiction, and she must have written as much to Mr. Doran, for he went on:

. . . If he was not addict[*sic*] at the time he entered the hospital, I
see no reason why he should be confined beyond the six months' period. However, if you feel that his addiction was of such a nature that
he needs to stay the full 18 months that is a decision that you will be
required to make.

A short time later Mother and Anne went to Lexington again, and
afterward Daddy wrote.

Dearest Hallie:

I hope that you and Anne arrived at home O.K. and did not have
any car trouble. . . . I have not had a visit from Mr. Doran since you
were here. . . . Has Anne come home to stay yet? I am so sorry that she
is giving up her schoolwork. I am terribly disappointed but there is
nothing I can do under the circumstances. I suppose I should be getting accustomed to disappointments by now tho since I have had so
many in the past. I am still living in Hope that maybe the future will
be some brighter. I want you to get the letters started to Washington
soon with a copy of each to this Institution (also get the same people to
write a different letter to Sen. Geo[rge] & Russell) send the letters to:
U.S. Parole Board—Dept. of Justice—Washington, D.C. Contact Ellis
A[rnall]. and Herman T[almadge]. and ask them to write letters—also
Ben F[ortson]. Start these as early as possible and work on the Q.T. Don't
let others know who all you intend to ask. . . . It is a very important
matter because I cannot do a thing in here—If it is not done on the
outside it will not be done—Do you believe me? If not please tell me so
in your next letter. Put off and delay and forgetfulness will not work in
this matter and it is most serious for me. All of the local letters that you
have sent in will help. . . . If Anne is at home she would be the proper
one to make the contacts and write the letters. Maybe her premature
decision will work to an advantage after all.

Love to all –

Wm. Henry Wall —

And so, under the double pressures of money and grave concern for Daddy's health, Mother and Anne launched a heavy campaign of letter-writing, enlisting as many people as possible to stump for an early release. Over the next several weeks Anne typed many letters, and as they got the campaign underway, Daddy wrote me:

Dear Son:

How are you getting along at school, etc. Fine I hope. I think of you every day and pray and wish that I could be with you—I am praying that you will be a good boy and I am sure you will, but please be careful with car and otherwise so you won't get hurt anyway—Daddy will be home sometime this year and I have some good plans for us. I intend to spend more time in trying to play and have fun with you as I see now it was useless to work so hard and take life and my obligations so seriously for nothing but pay interest unreasonable taxes and devote much time to charity—You remember the pretty Congressional Certificate of Merit that hung in the reception room of the Hospital. That was for free service and days on top of days that I gave my Govt. and Country during World War II—Of course I do not regret it and would do it again if necessary—But the rest of the Doctors there that are rejoicing in my absence at the present time did nothing like that— Our day will come again soon though and you can count on that—The great Creator and Master does not bless people that bears false witness against their neighbor –

I hope you will be able to read this letter and I don't make too many mistakes because I left my glasses in the room and I can't see very well . . . Son write to me soon and be a good boy and help Mother at Home.

Love Daddy — Wm. H. Wall —

It was a parent's letter to a very young child, not to an adolescent trying to be the man of the house. Another letter to Mother followed on February 4:

. . . I hope that you will carry out the instructions about the letters as I have asked you to and not wait *too late*—Don't use your imagination or let someone (that is not genuinely interested in my behalf) tell you a better way to do it. I have tried to be very specific in my request and suggestions. . . . I am very apprehensive about the final outcome of my business. For the 3rd time—*please send me some of my money.*

As ever, Wm. H. Wall —

Two weeks later:

. . . Of course before my trial I was confident I would be acquitted but I am thoroughly convinced that I can't take a thing for granted. I was also told that I probably wouldn't have to stay here long if I was not addicted—Never-the-less I have been incarcerated about 4_ months, the length of time designated as a cure by the Institution, and still I am in the dark about what time I will be fortunate enough to get out. I pray to God that it will be soon, though, because I can definitely see that the time is resting heavy and that no further "treatment" is necessary, and knowing a little about the practice of medicine I think I am in position to know.

Love — W. H. Wall

By that time we knew and Daddy understood that no treatment would ever be given, which is why he put the word in quotation marks. He wrote on February 26:

. . . The "cure" as designated by the Institution is 4_ months—Many Judges in the country give a probation sentence with the provision that the "patient" takes a "cure"—Then they are released to go home in 4 months and spend the rest of the sentence under probation—Like Mrs. Howell & Willie Mae!! My 4_ months will be up March 10th. It is already up if the time I spent in Camilla is added—But still I must wait until April before the parole officer comes from D.C. and then it will probably be May before I hear from the parole (If I am fortunate enough to make it). I am praying that I will!! I see so many people here with probation sentences and *many Doctors with no sentence at all* [emphasis added] but was given a chance to come here as a "volunteer" for 4_ months and the case closed.

When Mother showed me this letter I was surprised by his use of that word "volunteer." Until now no one had made such a point. He seemed to be saying that other physicians had been given the opportunity to "volunteer" for incarceration, with no criminal sentence on record. Daddy had no such luck.

In characteristically positive fashion he went on: "Well I suppose every thing will work out O.K. all hardships and inequalities will work themselves out eventually—" In the darkest circumstance his discouragement was balanced by his innate, energetic, positive approach to life.

His interest in politics continued, and he regularly read *Life* magazine along with *The Atlanta Journal* and *The Atlanta Constitution*:

> . . . I see that the U.S. Congress is trying to abolish poll tax all over the country—Other sections criticize Ga. as being a backward state but it seems Ga. sets the pace for rest of country [thanks to Gov. Arnall, Georgia had abolished its poll tax six years before]. Also Ike is asking that all 18 yrs. olds be allowed to vote—Ga. has had this 10 yrs.—Give Anne and Henry my love—I miss them so much—Write soon— Love—Daddy — Wm. H. Wall

The letter-writing campaign was bearing fruit. Many of those Mother or Anne had asked to write sent us copies of their letters to influential figures. Warren Mixon, a lawyer in Ocilla, wrote at Dr. Dismuke's request to Georgia's junior senator Richard Russell, whom he addressed as "Dick.":

> . . . There seems to be no doubt that Dr. Wall used some of the drug, but his friends feel that for him to have to serve a long term would probably destroy a great man in the medicine profession . . . upon investigation the Parole Board will find that Dr. Wall has not had

any drug since his conviction, and has not had even an aspirin tablet during his imprisonment. I would consider it a personal favor if you will take an interest in this case . . . and see if Dr. Wall can be paroled as soon as possible.

Senator Russell replied:

> Dear Warren: . . .
> Be assured that I shall be glad to do anything I can to be helpful to Dr. Wall and am getting in touch at once with the Chairman of the U. S. Board of Parole, urging that he be accorded every possible consideration. I hope that he will be released soon and will advise you further in a few days.

Mr. Ennis Fletcher, also of Ocilla, wrote to the Hon. Don Wheeler at the U.S. House of Representatives:

> Dr. Wall is a very fine and capable man in his profession [who] due to human weakness got off on the wrong foot during the last two or three years. . . . I will consider it a personal favor if you will take Dr. Wall's case up with the Parole Board there in Washington and do all you can to bring about his release. . . . If you are successful in this undertaking we do not feel that you will ever regret having helped this man.

A similar letter went from Mr. Philip Newbern of Ocilla to the state's senior senator, Walter George, also depicting Daddy as "a man of outstanding ability in his profession. . .a very fine Doctor."

Senator George replied, "I shall be pleased to contact the Board of Parole in an effort to be of assistance."

From Damascus, Georgia, H. C. and W. H. Haddock wrote to the U.S. Parole Board:

> We have known Dr. William Henry Wall for nineteen years and it gives us pleasure to recommend him unreservedly as a splendid physi-

cian. He has been greatly missed by the citizens of Early County, and we are merely the intermediary for numerous constituents of his when we earnestly ask you to allow him to return to Blakely in order that he can resume his practice.

Daddy's close friend, former governor Ellis Arnall, wrote:

> . . . I have known Dr. Wall very intimately for the past twenty years and have always regarded him as one of the finest citizens in our State. . . . I have been very closely associated with him [and] never seen any evidences which would lead me to the conclusion that he was or is a drug addict.
>
> Dr. Wall has been a civic leader in his community all his life; he has held high and responsible public offices; he has rendered excellent medical service to many, many patients; he has demonstrated in numerous ways the fact that he is a substantial and useful citizen.
>
> . . . At the time I had the honor to serve as Governor of Georgia (1943–1947), Dr. Wall was one of my leaders in the State Senate. So highly did I regard him as a professional man, a medical leader and outstanding citizen, that I appointed him a member of the Georgia State Board of Medical Examiners. In this capacity he rendered exemplary and meritorious service.
>
> I sincerely hope that when his application for parole is presented that you will find the circumstances and facts are such that favorable action will be given it.

Governor Arnall sent us the reply to his letter from George Anderson, Parole Officer in Lexington: ". . . Dr. Wall will become eligible for parole April 7, 1954, and his application will be considered . . . sometime during that month. . . . Dr. Wall's adjustment to our treatment program has been quite satisfactory and he will be informed of your interest in his behalf."

We had a wry laugh at that, knowing what comprised the "treatment program."

Letters of endorsement continued to pour in. O. F. Thompson wrote, as did H. A. Felder, who had gone on Daddy's bond. H. H. Sullivan, father of future U.S. Secretary of Health and Human Services Louis Sullivan, M.D., wrote. So did Sheriff C. C. "Tuck" Swann: "I think that the majority of the people in this town and county would be glad to see him return to his practice. . . . I personally will be glad to see him back at home." Sheriff Swann knew that in some quarters the old animosities were very much alive.

Bill Smith, Blakely's mayor pro-tem, wrote: "Dr. Wall enjoyed a good practice in Blakely and was considered by many to be the best doctor in Early County. I personally have known him for many years, and have liked him as a person and as a physician. I hope he will soon be allowed to return to Blakely and resume his practice."

Clarence E. Martin, Earl Beasley, and my close friend Clifford's father R. C. Singletary, Jr., wrote similar letters. J. B. Rice, my friend Charles's daddy, did as well. So did Mr. and Mrs. George Brown and cotton broker J. Carroll Rogers.

Adron Doran wrote to both Senator George and Senator Russell and received prompt replies promising their attention to Daddy's case. Mother wrote to Congressman J. L. Pilcher and was assured of his efforts on Daddy's behalf. After that, Anne and Mother spent several days driving all over South Georgia to see various people Daddy had asked them to see.

"I have known Doctor Wall for thirty years," Representative Pilcher wrote to the Parole Board. "He has always been an outstanding citizen and doctor in his community. . . . His many friends in Georgia, and I as a life-long friend, would be very grateful if his parole could be granted when he becomes eligible."

Secretary of State Ben Fortson wrote:
> I have known Dr. Wall intimately for many years. He and I served together in the General Assembly of Georgia and have been close personal friends for a long time. I know him well. He is a splendid doctor, a man of fine character, and deserves an opportunity. I sincerely hope that it

will be possible for him to be paroled at the earliest possible moment.

Whatever mistake he may have made will only make him a better citizen and a better doctor. I have complete confidence in him and utmost respect for him.

Reading these letters made us all feel a little better. Why, of so many outstanding friends, had such a few come forward in support at the time of the trial? Had the arrest and federal charges come as such a great shock to everyone except Daddy's betrayers that no one else believed he would ever be convicted?

Meanwhile I was trying to go on with my life. Daphner had warmed up a little, and without Daddy needing the car for house calls, from time to time Mother let me drive it for dates.

Whenever I was with Daphner I could actually think about a future when times would be happy. It might be years away, but she helped me to believe it could happen.

Baseball season started, and I went out for the team. Daddy wrote to Mother:

> . . . Tell Henry that I saw about him going out for the baseball team in the *Albany Herald* this week. I get the *Herald* from another man here. . . . I hope he will be able to make the team and I am sure he will—Tell him to work hard and he will make it in a big way. I hope something can be worked out about the nurses' home. I hope that I will be able to buy it (even though it will cost $6,500) as I feel sure I could get that much out of it anytime in the future. In fact I probably could get even more than that—Holland would give more just to keep me out—That is why I was so insistent on staying quiet on the matter. . . . I can see that many were in the dark either *ignorantly* or *on purpose* in advising me . . . I suppose the Spring weather is pretty down there. It is still cold and dreary here. I will certainly be glad to put my foot on Early Co. soil again.

Either Mother or Anne must have floated the suggestion of Anne's coming up to Kentucky to be married, so that he could be present. He wrote back:

> Was glad to hear from you. I am sorry that I cannot tell you when I will be able to be with you at Home—Of course I would like to be there when you and "Jiggs" get married. You see the Parole Board will have interviews here this month but the date of the month seems to vary from time to time. Then if I am fortunate to make parole it will take some time for final clearance. I do not think it practical at all for you to come here for wedding—That is out! . . . All I can suggest is that you use your own Judgement—and do what you think best—Remembering that Marriage is a long game. Sometimes it is very happy and others it is very detrimental. Since you are so bent on it before you finish your college work I truly hope yours will be happy. I am so sorry that I won't be there as it is very doubtful that I will be there anytime during April. I have not seen Mr. Doran for three weeks now. I hope he will come to see me tomorrow. Tell all the people that I appreciate the letters and truly hope that none in the negative are sent in—Of course you won't know about them—I am not afraid of any that would cover the full details and tell the full truth instead of a libelous half truth. I sincerely believe that I have honestly and conscientiously served society and all humanity of Early Co. equally as well if not better than any Doctor that has ever lived in Early Co. both past and present. I know without a doubt that I have put more in it than anyone else—But it seems all that matters is the Dollars & cents you have in the Bank. Instead of putting it in the Bank I put it in a Hospital for someone else to use and benefit by—Well that is all in life—All I can do now is look to the future without a spark of bitterness in my heart and mind. I feel sorry for those that have crooked and sinned against me. Hope that the Lord will forgive them. Write to me again soon darling as I love you so much. Tell Henry to write. I love him and wish I could be with both of you.

Letters continued to pour in endorsing Daddy's parole: our minister, Mr. McKibben, wrote a letter in March. Julian J. Moore asked Congressman Pilcher for help: "We need a Doctor of Dr. Wall's charitable feelings for the Poor in need of Medical attention that at present are not getting due to the large amounts charged by the Doctors here in Blakely." Stewart Chandler wrote. So did D. C. "Babe" Morgan. Oscar Whitchard, former State Representative Leon H. Baughman, and Governor Herman Talmadge.

A FEW WEEKS before Anne's wedding, Mother embarrassed Anne, Jiggs, and me again. "E. B.," she said, "now that you're getting ready to be a member of this family, I'm sure you won't mind my asking you to lend me some money toward the costs of the wedding. I need about two hundred dollars." She didn't even look ashamed to be asking.

E. B. put a hand up to his face, squeezed both cheeks at once, then said, "I'm so sorry, Mrs. Wall. I wish I had it to lend you, but I've been saving up so Anne and I can get married, and I barely have enough to see us through the first couple of months."

"Is that so?" Mother said. "Well, it didn't hurt to ask."

Reluctantly, Mother saw that she would have to arrange a quiet wedding at home. Anne was already sewing her own wedding dress. I felt sad that Daddy wouldn't be there, but what could I do?

DICK DISMUKE reported that Dr. Holland had agreed to buy the hospital, at a bargain-basement price. That would be a bitter blow for Daddy, but we understood that Dr. Dismuke deserved to recoup as much of the money he and his friends had put out on our behalf as he could. At least the residents of the county would still have a hospital, though the Walls no longer had any say-so about how it was to be run.

At the end of March we learned that a parole hearing was scheduled on April 13 and that if parole were recommended, several more weeks could pass before it took effect.

Mother quickly sent off one final plea:

> . . . When you review this trial, you will learn that he had in his employ two admitted addicts. These people have been allowed to remain

at home on probation while Dr. Wall has been forced to serve time and take full responsibility for them all.

We, his family, during this period have suffered untold embarrassment as well as financial losses. The fact that he was incarcerated has resulted in the loss of approximately $150,000 worth of property. Had this property not been bought by a friend, we would have been entirely penniless and homeless. This friend has recently resold property at a great sacrifice and personal loss to himself.

We will appreciate it very much if his application for parole can be granted at the earliest possible date . . . He is badly needed at home by his family and patients. Our only daughter is to be married on the 24th of April, and it would mean very much to him to be at home on that day.

While Daddy was slow to acknowledge Mother's efforts, her resolve to get our family finances on a more stable basis never let up. As promised, Dr. Dismuke and his friends conveyed the deed to our house to her, subject to a five thousand dollar loan, on the condition that she make a regular payment of fifty-five dollars the first of every month. Her struggle was beginning to pay off.

From Lexington Daddy reported a new assignment, doing stoop labor on the grounds of the superintendent's house and keeping weeds out of a strawberry patch. He must have chosen the outdoor work, because he was always a farm boy at heart and enjoyed growing things. Still, I couldn't imagine his portly presence bending over those rows of plants in the hot spring sun. To me, it seemed humiliating for one who had so recently acted and moved among the most influential people of our state.

About this time Mother had a letter from a physician in Vienna, Georgia, that really lifted our spirits. Here was somebody who cared and understood:

Dear Mrs. Wall,

I have been on Senator [Walter] George's coattail ever since I saw you, concerning Dr. Wall. I saw Heard George this last week personally,

they have taken it up with the authorities frequently. Heard tells me he is
due home now pretty soon. We all know what the trouble is and where
it all origanated [sic]. Sid Howell as you well know is responsible for all
the trouble. In fact he has his bill in everything that does not concern
him from all reports I get. When the Dr. comes home I want to see him
as quick as possible. Hope everything is all right with you all and he will
soon be home. . . . With best wishes . . . V. C. Daves, M.D.

Over those spring months Congressman Pilcher was the point man
who responded most often and most strenuously to the myriad requests
to bring Daddy home. We couldn't understand why he'd been held in
prison longer than was usual for such cases, unless it was because the
doctors in charge of the "experiments" wanted to watch for long-term
effects of whatever drug had been administered covertly to him. On April
30, 1954, we received his telegram saying the Parole Board had granted
parole effective May 15—three weeks after Anne's wedding date.

In one way it was a huge relief to know he was being released; in
another it brought fresh anxieties. What would he be like when he came
home? Could he regain sufficient medical practice to make a living? Would
people stay away for fear he was still using drugs? Would he find enemies
lying in wait at every turn? All we could do was pray and trust.

I believed that while he was gone I had truly grown up, no longer the
immature child Daddy thought he was writing to, I knew things would
never be as they once were between us, yet I had to trust we could find
our way to a companionable friendship.

Someone has said, "Be careful what you pray for." For months I had
prayed feverishly for Daddy's safe return. I might not have prayed so
specifically had I known just what his return would bring with it.

Chapter 8

After that things started happening fast. Anne and E. B. were married at our house and left after a small reception to set up housekeeping in Bainbridge, where E. B. worked. Little more than a week later we received a special-delivery airmail letter (postage twenty-six cents) from Lexington.

> Dear Mrs. Wall,
>
> I went to see Dr. Wall last night. He is in fine spirits. They report that he will be released at midnight Friday, May 14. I will meet him and bring him to our house and get a plane for him on Saturday May 15, for Atlanta. He asked that I send you this $500 check. You can endorse it to the banker or he can hold it as security against the loan in good faith until Dr. Wall gets home. I know you all are anxious about his return.
>
> Yours sincerely,
> Adron Doran

Less than a month before he wrote that letter and made those arrangements to help Daddy and Mother, Mr. Doran had been elected president of Morehead State College. It's quite a tribute to his character that in the first flush of his new responsibilities he did not forget someone who needed his help. Very few of us can claim such admirable friends.

On May 7 we received a last letter from Daddy:

> I wrote for the Ins. Loan and I hope it arrives before I leave as I will need it—Tell Henry I will come on plane—I will call or wire when I want you to meet me when I learn schedule—I will probably arrive on 16th or thereabout. . . . I am real anxious to see you all and hope to

hear from you soon—I hope to see Mr. Doran Sat. a.m. 15th—In fact he has promised to meet me here on my release. Be sure to have my clothes cleaned and in good order as I want to see my friends in Route and when I arrive home.

Love,

HenryWilliam Henry Wall

The day we had all been praying and waiting for came. Anne and E. B. came from Bainbridge to help us welcome Daddy, and I drove her and Mother to the Albany airport to meet the plane from Atlanta. We had just parked the car and walked inside the building to wait when I spotted Daddy's old arch-enemy, dressed in a suit and talking to some other man.

"My God, you all, there's Sid Howell! He knew Daddy was on his way and came down here to kill him."

Anne said in a low voice, "You all wait here. I'm calling the Albany police. They need to get out here quick to stop a murder." Before I could say anything, she scurried away.

Mother grabbed my arm. "Hush, son, don't look at him. Come on, we'll walk out of his sight and get a Coke. Don't you think he could be here for some other reason?"

"Don't you believe it. He hates Daddy, and I don't trust the old crook." I kept my eye on him. Howell wasn't our county's all-powerful sheriff any more, but I'd have bet a hundred dollars he packed a pistol under that coat. He looked just the same—scrawny, that ever-present cigarette drooping from the corner of his mouth.

At last the DC-3 landed and taxied to the gate. The ground crew rolled the movable stairs out to the plane, and when the door opened we watched for Daddy's familiar shape. A half-dozen people got off and came down the steps—still no Daddy.

Sid and the man with him moved up to the tarmac fence. The stranger carried a briefcase, and anything could have been in it. Had Sid hired a hit man? I was wishing I'd brought Daddy's .38 when the stranger shook Sid's hand, picked up his briefcase, and walked out to the plane. My heart seemed to stop. Was he going after Daddy? The last emerging passenger came down the steps, then seemed to recognize the stranger waiting at the foot of the steps and stopped to speak.

When I looked around frantically for Sid he was walking rapidly to the parking lot. If murder was to be done, Sid wouldn't witness it or be the one to do it. Just then Anne came running up, pointed, called out, "Look, it's Daddy!" and rushed toward that last arrival. I had to look twice, then look again. The man I saw looked like Daddy's ghost.

"Dear heaven!" Mother grabbed my arm, then managed a wave. "What in the world have they done to him? Henry! Over here!"

Anne clung to him as he walked toward us. It really was Daddy, I could see that now, though his bulk had shrunk by a third. The suit he had on was cheap and ill-fitting, and even though his color looked healthy from outdoor work, the flesh hung loose on his neck and deep lines crisscrossed his face.

What in God's name had happened to him? I did my best to wipe the shock off my face and replace it with a smile. And then he was in our midst, exchanging hugs and kisses and words of relief.

When I managed to clear my throat enough to speak, I said, "Daddy, who was that man you spoke to out at the plane?"

"A lobbyist I knew from when I was in the senate."

"Did you see who came to put him on the plane?"

"No, I was too busy searching for you all. Who was it?"

"Sid Howell. We thought he'd come down here to kill you."

"Huh! Not old Sid. He wouldn't do it at the airport in broad daylight. He'd find some underhanded way. Don't worry, I'll be ready for whatever he tries."

Poor Daddy looked so old and puny I doubted he was ready for anybody.

"You look good, Daddy," Anne said. "You've lost a lot of weight."

I didn't think he looked good at all. I thought he looked like he'd been starved nearly to death.

He sniffed. "You would, too, living on soup and water. Thirty more pounds and Doctor Davison'll get his wish."

Mother said, "Well, we can't have you looking like a scarecrow. We've got a real good supper planned, pot roast with vegetables."

He attempted a grin. "Reckon this little shriveled-up belly can take it?"

He insisted on a good meal at a nearby restaurant we were familiar with. We all had a delicious dinner and a round of drinks. It was the first time he and E. B. had met. Daddy was most gracious and in good spirits. Several people from Blakely who happened to be in the restaurant came over and welcomed him home. The homecoming seemed off to a good start.

THAT NIGHT it felt great to have him back in the house and hear those gentle snores issue from his room. Unable to switch off my churning thoughts, I lay in bed and tried to fall asleep, then finally tuned my little Zenith to my old comfort—WWL and Dixieland jazz. With Daddy home the world seemed safer, but I knew our troubles were far from done.

Many things had to be worked out before we could expect some semblance of the life that used to be. Daddy finally understood the disposition of his property: as for the hospital, Dr. Holland had bought it and intended running it, while Dick Dismuke was holding the nurses' residence for Daddy's use. Although he said he was eager to get back to work, I could tell how much he hated knowing that his long-standing, less competent rival was ensconced next door in what had been *his* hospital.

"Listen, Daddy," I said, "I know it's a hard blow, seeing Dr. Holland get your hospital."

He made a wry face. "I can't say I like the idea. That so-and-so sitting at my fine desk, it just about eats me up." But then he chuckled, and that old twinkle came back to his eye. "Holland got a little surprise, you know. When Dick divided the property he told the surveyor to run the line smack down the middle of the drive. So now Holland can't get the ambulance up to his emergency room."

A FULL-TIME OPENING to teach third and fourth grade arose, and Mother took it. Her increased income did not end the friction over money between her and Daddy. Right up to his incarceration he'd been totally in charge of family finances. Mother had been forced to take over and do her best. Rather than compliment her, he seemed to resent it. I think really he was frustrated and terribly disappointed in himself. She'd carried us through the worst, done what she could to help make up for his past mistakes. Maybe he was surprised, like me, to discover that iron core of resolve in the wife to whom he'd written "Silly thing!"

Then, too, Dick and his friends had pulled our family chestnuts out of the fire, and while all of us were immensely grateful to them, instead of berating himself for letting things get to that point, Daddy took his sense of failure out on Mother, the woman who'd stuck by him through it all. The wonder-worker of former days couldn't get comfortable with his demotion. He found it easy to see himself as a victim, because so many antagonists and circumstances had conspired against him. We were beginning to see that his months in Lexington had done something to his spirit that wasn't likely to come undone.

IN DADDY'S ABSENCE, Juanita had done any little job that came along, from picking cotton to helping Mother with housework, though Mother could pay her only a pittance. When Daddy told her he wanted her back as his medical assistant, Juanita just beamed.

"Don't you worry, Doctor Wall. I'll help you, and don't mind about paying me, either. Ernest and me, we're doing all right. We'll make out till you can pay."

Daddy enlisted Ernest to help me move what he needed into his new quarters, and Juanita helped set up the place for seeing patients. That abandoned desk still bothered him; we reminded him again that we couldn't move it, and anyway, we'd had no place to store it. All his fine top-of-the-line stainless-steel equipment had gone with the hospital, to be replaced by pitiful secondhand stuff—chipped enamel basins and white-painted iron stands—all showing evidence of hard wear. He started out with high hopes nevertheless and ordered a new sign for the entrance—Wall Clinic—to let people know he was open for practice again.

Whenever Mother urged him to take it easy and rest from these exertions, he bucked. "Listen here, Hallie, don't you know I need something to do? You ought to realize, the sooner I get back in practice, the sooner we'll get out of this mess." He clearly expected to be the breadwinner again soon.

Gradually a few patients drifted in, nothing like his former steady stream. He couldn't stop fretting.

"I ought to be doing better by now," he kept saying.

ONE SATURDAY NIGHT late our phone rang at home. Daddy went to answer it, and from the living room I could hear the conversation.

"Who told you to call me?" he said. "Why won't you say? . . . Anyhow, what made you think I'd ever do such a thing? . . . No, I don't care what you pay me, I'm not about to do it." He slammed down the phone, came back in the living room, and sat down to read.

He said no more about the call, and something told me not to ask, though I kept wondering. What could the request have been? Eventually it came to me. Somebody who knew he was hard up for money had called to ask him to get rid of an unwanted pregnancy—a thing Daddy would never have done. At the hospital he'd sometimes performed a D & C—a necessary uterine dilatation and curettage after a miscarriage—but he adored children and would never have terminated a viable life.

HE RELISHED his meals, though at times he would just sit and stare silently out a window. Did Early County soil feel as grand as he'd dreamed up there in Kentucky? I offered to take him out for a drive, or let him drive and just ride along, but he said no, he wanted to enjoy being at home and looking forward to work.

As a condition of his release he'd had to designate some responsible local person as his parole advisor; he chose D. M. Carter. When Mr. Carter came by to see him I couldn't figure out why Mother seemed so uneasy—until she floored me by confiding that while Daddy was gone he'd accused her of carrying on an affair with the man. It was an absurd suggestion. I knew Mr. Carter for an upright, God-fearing, entirely respectable person. And Mother, who'd always kept so much to herself? How could she have carried on an affair when she was working night and day to make ends meet? If Daddy truly believed his own accusation, choosing this man made no sense.

Either Daddy had never believed it or he'd forgotten his accusation, because he said after Mr. Carter left, "That man and Adron Doran have both done so much for us, I want us to join that Church of Christ. You can't deny the Methodists sure let us down."

Mother didn't answer until he pressed her. "Now how would that look, Henry, an organist and piano teacher in that little church that's opposed to all instrumental music?"

He waved a dismissive hand. "Brother Carter and Brother Doran are such fine men, I can't see letting a thing like that stand in our way." I noticed he'd adopted their denomination's form of address. "Why, nobody would give it a thought."

"Well, I'm sorry, but that's how I feel. You do as you please."

We didn't join the Church of Christ. As for Daddy, he had never been a regular with the Methodists, and Mother and I weren't such Methodist regulars ourselves.

School let out for the summer, and with no hospital responsibilities I told Mr. Carter I was ready for the factory job. He set me to work building grain elevators—long mechanized belts that could move grain from a truck into a bin or silo. The job paid minimum wage, one dollar an hour, up from the previous summer's seventy-five cents at Kolomoki Park.

The welding skills I'd learned for an FFA project stood me in good stead now. Nobody had told me to wear safety goggles, and I was hammering flux off a weld when a fragment flew up to lodge in my eye. It hurt like the dickens until our EENT specialist Dr. Rhyne got the fragment out. I was mighty grateful when it healed and my eye was spared. From that point on, I was taking care of myself in a sense, paying for my clothes and other needs with the money I made and saving what I could.

During those long hot days at work my thoughts kept running back to Daddy's promise to spend more time with me. It made me sad, because the promise came too late. In the past he'd been swamped with work; now I was the one who was too busy. The happy era of Dr. Wall and his shadow Little Doc was over for good.

At night when I came home worn out he was always there, morose and moody, at loose ends after a day of waiting for patients who rarely came. No longer the fun-loving Daddy I had known. After weeks of it he moved a recliner chair and a television into his medical office so he could sit at ease while he waited, watch whatever came on, read, or now and again just doze off. What a pathetic comedown from a packed waiting room, a long roster of house calls, and a hospital full of folks needing his care.

WE GOT SOMETHING new to worry about when Daddy adopted a fresh consolation. While he'd never been a big drinker, he'd always enjoyed a drink or two in congenial company. Early County had no legal sales of hard liquor at the time—owing, some said, to the preachers and the bootleggers—but there were a half-dozen beer joints around. Daddy began keeping beer at the house to drink and got in the habit, out of boredom and loneliness, of dropping in at Mode Stinson's beer joint downtown as well.

Telling his jokes and enjoying the company revived his old congeniality, but it dissipated the minute he was back at the house. We never saw him frankly drunk, but he would go off to his room or his bathroom, and when he came out it was often obvious he'd had a few beers, because he'd be touchier and more depressed. Mother and I just prayed it was a stage that would pass.

A friend of mine worked in the same block as Mode Stinson's place, and after one of those long afternoons when no patients had come, he gave me an eyewitness report of a dramatic encounter. Daddy had driven downtown, stopping at Mode's, and ordered a beer. He was sitting at the bar taking his first sip when another customer walked over and sat on the stool beside him. It was Sid Howell, half-lit and loaded for bear.

"Say, Wall"—he jabbed a finger at Daddy's face—"I've got a bone to pick with you. You're the very one, goddammit, that got my son's wife

Jane hooked on dope. She's left him, and you're the cause of it all."

Daddy said, "You got that wrong, Sid. The woman was an addict before she ever came to work for me. Ask the folks over in Edison, they know all about it."

Sid narrowed his eyes against the smoke of his cigarette. "You're a damn liar."

Fighting words. Daddy, never one to back away from a challenge, had always told me, "Son, if you have to hit somebody, don't write him a letter first," and he practiced what he preached. Didn't even draw back, just popped Sid's head with his beer bottle so hard that Sid fell off his stool and hit the floor like a sawed-off Georgia pine. Heedless of the blood spurting from Sid's forehead, Daddy lit into his old enemy with fists flying as if he meant to kill the man.

The nearest customers grabbed him. "Hold on here, Doc!" Mode came out from behind the bar to lend a hand as Sid fumbled in his trouser pocket and scrambled to find his feet.

Daddy was doing his best to shake them off. "My God, don't hold me and let that S.O.B. shoot me!"

But they wouldn't turn loose, and when a stunned and staggering Sid brought his hand out of his trouser pocket it wasn't a pistol he held, but the keys to his car.

"Come on, Sid," somebody said. "We got to get you to the doctor, get that head sewed up."

Daddy straightened up and adjusted his tie. "Bastard called me a liar."

"Better drop it," Mode said.

Sid put a hand to his head, then stared at the blood. "Goddamn you, Wall. I'll be back directly to fix you."

A couple of men walked Sid outside, put him in his car, and drove him off to Cuthbert to get his head sewn up.

At that point in his life I think Daddy felt he had nothing else to lose. In years past he'd carried a pistol in his car only when he went out at night on house calls, but after Lexington he always kept one close by. That day he went out to his own car, got behind the steering wheel, opened the glove box with the pistol in easy reach, and sat there with his door open and one foot on the curb. My friend telling the story said the beer-joint customers went to laying bets on how long Daddy would live, convinced that Sid would come back and finish him off.

As it was, after an uneventful hour, Daddy went back to his office and told Juanita all about it, then came on home at the end of the day. Nothing more of the fracas was heard. Sid never filed charges. He'd provoked the attack and perhaps realized that his adversary no longer valued his own life. Daddy's first violent episode in Blakely was far from his last, but all the others would take place within the walls of our own home.

AT THE END of that tense summer came the horrible night after the baseball game when he truly went mad. I understood then that some part of his brain had been damaged, and how profound the damage must be. Barely recovering from the previous school year's despair and depression, I was plunged back into them more deeply than ever. On top of everything else, my father had gone insane.

I tortured myself with questions. Could someone be crazy for one night and not crazy for good? Daddy had a mentally compromised nephew—could the same illness be turning up in him? Scared as I was, I told myself that couldn't be so, because crazy people were crazy all the time, not just now and again. Some other dreadful thing was wrong, and I had no idea what it was.

From time to time after that middle-of-the-night combat, I would see a frightened, piercing expression come over Daddy's face—for no discernible reason. He seemed to be seeing or hearing something nobody else could see or hear. I came to know that look all too well, for it might appear at any time, in any situation. It was like keeping company with a time bomb, and whenever he walked into a room with me I feared the bomb might go off.

THAT AUTUMN he applied for a return to good standing in the Medical Association of Georgia, and since nobody outside the family knew of his persistent dysfunction, arrangements were made through the local

Tri-County Society to grant him a probationary year. During it he would pay no dues, would not be able to vote or hold office, and would have to answer to a senior member. When the start of the probationary year was made retroactive to the date of his conviction, Daddy appreciated his colleagues' vote of confidence. His supervision would run only a few months, to be followed by a return to full membership. We prayed that nothing would go wrong, for even limited participation in the medical fold lifted his spirits.

With his Georgia license in the balance, he still had to go to Atlanta to answer to the Board of Medical Examiners—the same panel on which he had so recently sat, in the capitol building where he'd served with pride. The board allowed him to keep his license. One more hurdle overcome.

THE WELCOME RELIEF of football season ushered in my senior high school year. When I was named co-captain of the team, I had solid reason to hold up my head again. Daddy, with plenty of time on his hands, showed up for every game. Coach Summerhill had moved on, and while our new coach, Mr. Buckner, wasn't the same heartwarming kind of friend, he did lead us to a super season. When we played Dawson High School, Coach Summerhill traveled from his new location to watch; we won, and his compliments on how well I'd played meant the world to me. My spirits got still another lift when, at season's end, I was the only Georgia player picked for the All-Wiregrass Team.

Our life was settling down to some semblance of stability when Daddy told us that something peculiar was happening to his mail. He always received a big pile of mail—bills, letters, drug samples, journals, correspondence of all kinds. Lately, he said, every item addressed to him had clearly been opened and resealed before being delivered. He went down to the post office, hot under the collar, to straighten things out. The encounter, as he reported it to Mother and me, was mystifying.

"Look here," he told Mr. Houston, our postmaster, "somebody's been opening my mail."

Mr. Houston didn't seem at all surprised.

Daddy said, "Well, aren't you going to stop it, find out who's doing it?"

Mr. Houston shrugged. "I know who's doing it and why, but I can't tell you. It's out of my hands."

"Out of your hands? Come on, man, you're in charge here."

"I'm sorry." That was all Mr. Houston would say.

That night Daddy told us, "He knows what's going on. Some high muckety-muck put the screws to him, told him to keep his mouth shut or lose his job."

Just because you're paranoid, some wit has said, doesn't mean they're not out to get you. In Daddy's case somebody in our own government was monitoring my daddy's mail, and that was a truly scary thing. It went on like that for months, and we never found out why, or who was responsible.

ANNE CAME HOME fairly often from Bainbridge to visit, and Daddy talked to her about his Lexington experiences, wanting her to write them up. He was bitter and critical of what passed for care at the so-called hospital, and particularly bitter at being labeled paranoid. Who wouldn't be paranoid, he said, with political enemies gunning for him, competitors out to bring his practice down, federal authorities seizing his hospital and selling his home out from under him, employees betraying him in federal court, and unidentified persons snooping through his mail? On top of all that, the government's doctors charged with his care had dosed him, *against his will*, with some unknown substance that had robbed him of all confidence in his sanity. No wonder he felt persecuted.

As for his fellow prisoners, he told us he'd been "hospitalized"—a scornful laugh at the word—with a bunch of hardened criminals. He now had quite a repertoire of stories about the underworld characters he'd come to know. Convicted killers, mobbed-up types who kept him informed of organized-crime hits all over the country—in Tampa's Ybor City, New York, Chicago, California. Some of those people scared him so much that he'd been afraid to be on an elevator with them. There was even a Hollywood actress named Lila Leeds who, along with actor Robert Mitchum, had been convicted of some drug offense.

"I'm just a country doctor, you know," he told Anne, "and in my wildest imagination I could never have pictured being thrown with such people, much less rubbing elbows with them every day. It was truly surreal."

He particularly emphasized how he despised Harris Isbell. "People still speak with loathing of that Nazi doctor, Josef Mengele—the one who carried out such horrible experiments on Jewish prisoners. Well, as far as I'm concerned, Isbell's the American Mengele. He's a disgrace, and the public who pay his salary ought to be told how evil the man is."

He definitely had a story he felt should be told, but Anne was young, absorbed in her own new family, which now included a baby son, and she couldn't undertake to help.

By now I was deeply in love with Daphner, and we were already talking about post-graduation plans. She intended to enter nursing school in Atlanta, while I aimed for a medical career, well aware that I would have to attend a state-supported school. Even that would be a financial strain, but I resolved to make it happen. From Atlanta to the University of Georgia was only sixty miles, and I didn't want to be a mile further from Daphner than I could help.

ONE-DAY THAT WINTER, Daddy had been acting crazy—no longer a rare event. He was at odds with Mother over some inconsequential thing and swung back and forth between silent brooding and wild, irrational talk. By evening I was doing homework in my front bedroom and trying to stay out of his way. Mother, also keeping her distance, was busy elsewhere in the house. For weeks he'd been even more morose than usual, and nothing anybody said or did seemed to help.

It was a cold night, and I watched him go out to the car in his shirtsleeves. When I saw the look on his face when he came back in a minute later, I knew for sure that things had suddenly turned bad. He went straight to his room without saying a word, and I knew he'd been to the car to retrieve his .38 Special snub-nosed revolver—always loaded.

The only sound in the house came from the kitchen, the refrigerator's low hum. How I knew it I can't say, but he intended to kill himself.

I couldn't just sit there and wait to hear the shot. I had to get the pistol away from him, but how? I got up, slipped off my shoes, eased down the hall, and peeked from the shadowy hall into his room. He hadn't seen or heard me. He was standing by the bed, and I could see the pistol's bulge in his pants pocket. Praying for luck to hold, when he turned his back I slipped in behind him, darted my hand into that pocket, and seized the gun.

He was far too quick for me. He whirled around, and with both hands grabbed my hand with the gun in it.

"Dammit, turn it loose! Get away from me!"

"I'm not turning it loose." I needed every ounce of strength to keep my death-hold on that loaded pistol, waving crazily between us in the air as we struggled for what felt like forever. I had my finger outside the trigger guard, but anything could happen.

I braced myself, then gave a sudden jerk.

"Let me have it, before it goes off!"

He gripped me like a vise. "GET OUT OF HERE! This is none of your business!"

"It *is* my business. I won't let you do what you're trying to do!"

He seemed superhumanly strong. I held onto the gun till my hand went numb, coaxing him, trying to calm him, persuade him to let go. Finally, at the very moment when I feared I couldn't hang on a second longer, he relaxed his hold.

The breath just streamed out of my lungs. "Okay. Thank you."

I pressed the catch to swing the cylinder away from the barrel and ejected the bullets into my hand. "I'm carrying this to put it where you won't be tempted to use it."

Even as I said it I knew he had other means of doing away with himself, because he kept three other revolvers, two shotguns, and two rifles in his closet. Fortunately the self-destructive urge seemed to have passed.

But he was still mad, still morose. He glared at me and said, "Well,

W. H. Wall, M.D., circa 1960, experiencing flashback.
Note expressionless stare.

I'm leaving," then stormed out of the house, got in the car, and drove
off. I raced outside to follow on my Harley, and when I saw him check
into the local motel, decided he was all right and went home.

The crisis was over. As I wheeled the Harley around to put it away,
my hands shook as if palsied and my legs felt like spaghetti. It was a
close, extremely scary call—so scary I couldn't tell anybody what had
happened. And the most awful part was knowing the same thing could

happen again at any time.

Next morning before breakfast he walked calmly into my room and said, "Listen, son, I want you to know how really sorry I am about last night."

Mother and I had grown used to the apologies that followed his crazy spells, but however sincere they seemed, they never took away the anguish or the fear.

Flustered, I was trying to collect my books for school. "It's okay, Daddy. Don't worry about it."

"Well, I do worry. I can't help feeling mighty bad. Whatever they gave me in Lexington really messed me up. That wasn't me, acting like that. You know it, don't you, son?"

"Yes sir, I know. It's all right. Just let it ride."

A few days later he handed me a photo somebody had taken of him in the back of Howell's Drugstore. He'd had his hat on indoors, which was odd, and one glance at that alienated mask told me he'd been in one of those horrid states. Whoever took the picture must have seen it. Did the photographer have any idea of what it meant? It was a godawful secret to keep.

GLAD FOR THE ADVENT OF SPRING, I went out again for baseball. High school sports to me meant camaraderie, accomplishment, and strenuous physical exertion that shoved my worries to the back of my mind. On my way home from practice I often dropped by Daddy's office to find him just sitting, waiting, doing little or nothing. Juanita was always there, keeping his records, sterilizing instruments, tidying the rooms. They'd set up a separate room for obstetrical deliveries, and if it looked as though the labor was going to be a long one, Juanita might sit with the mother and let Daddy go home overnight, then call him back when the baby was about to be born. If he didn't make it in time or wasn't in any state to come, I suspect that Juanita actually delivered some of those babies herself, and she would have done an excellent job. When nothing else was happening she listened patiently to his complaints about Mother and me, refuting his preposterous accusations in her kind and gentle way.

It can't be denied that long before the troubles began, relations between Daddy and Mother were strained. At first theirs had been a true romance, sorely tested as time passed by Daddy's addiction and the crash that followed. Now they were at odds most of the time, and late in the evenings the friction between them seemed to intensify.

One night when after some heated words he couldn't find the car keys, he went stomping out of the house and struck out walking toward downtown. I got in the car and followed, inching along beside him, begging him to let me drive him home. He wasn't himself at all, and when he walked up onto the front porch of Son Jones's house, I figured he was fixing to get shot. I got out of the car and managed to coax him away, yet even after he gave in, he refused to come home and insisted on spending another night at the motel.

That night I knew he had no gun with him, but on other nights I couldn't be sure. Juanita told me that all during that terrible time, on the mornings when she came to work and saw his car parked outside; she was always terrified she would come inside to find he'd done away with himself during the night.

And all the while Mother and I were struggling to keep our misery a secret from the rest of the town. A few people had to know things weren't right—the motel manager, for one. We hoped he just saw it as a rocky marriage. I believe only the family and Juanita knew how profound his derangement was, and Juanita was and still is the soul of discretion. Her loyalty kept her at his side; her compassion for him touched his heart.

The closer I got to the end of high school, the more excited I grew about leaving home for college. People kept saying, "I bet you'll be graduating with high honors like your sister." I tried to laugh it off, because the turmoil of the past two years had knocked my grades for a loop. My biggest challenge would be figuring out how to get the money to see me through college. Nobody could call me lazy, because from the age of thirteen I'd worked every chance I got, beginning with that tractor-repair project for the FFA, then going on to the hospital, half a dozen more little jobs in between, the backbreaker at Kolomoki, and finally at Mr. Carter's plant.

After graduation I went straight to work again, first a bread route, then a better job driving a dump truck on a road-paving project. At the end of my first day on the job I'd hauled the last truckload of gravel to the spot where the paving was going on when the foreman told me they didn't need any more gravel there.

"Just raise that body halfway up," he told me, "then go back real slow along the edge of the whole section we've paved today. We'll get a shovel in behind you and spread gravel on spots that still need a little more."

I did as he said, and after I finished one side he told me to turn around and go back along the other. With the body of that truckload of gravel still halfway up, I looked for a place to turn around, and when I backed to the edge of the road and hit the brake I thought the truck felt kind of light on the front end. I meant to put it in double-low gear to go forward, but missed double-low and went clear to reverse, promptly backing all the way into the ditch. And by the time I found double-low and gunned that Chevrolet dump truck with eight thousand pounds of gravel in the back, the body just raised straight up in the air. I looked out my window to discover the front wheels eight feet off the ground.

When I pushed the lever to let the body down, thinking the truck would come down with it, the front end went all the way up to meet the body instead. So there I was, like a man sitting on the nose cone of a rocket. And all the time the gravel was falling out the back—and after the whole load fell out, the truck with me in it slammed back to the ground, the rear end still firmly stuck in the ditch.

Oh my God, I thought, I'll never get to keep this job. I was mortified. The boss man wasn't there, just the foreman and the rest of the crew, and of course they were laughing fit to kill. Finally they brought a tractor, hooked a chain on it, and pulled the truck out. I was thinking, man, I'm out of here, but they kept me on. At least after that I knew some more things that I could and couldn't do. And through the whole incident I hadn't given one thought to Daddy or the troubles at home.

Chapter 9

That summer I saved every cent for college I could, but when the time came to go I had to borrow more from the Trust Company of Georgia to pay my bills. Being in Athens was like having a blessing in one hand and a curse in the other. In one sense I felt the weight of the world lifted from my shoulders, yet the home situation was always foremost in my mind. And Daphner was sixty miles away in Atlanta, while there I was in Athens with no car. She and I wrote letters back and forth constantly and talked on the phone now and then; I missed her like crazy and looked for any chance of a ride to Atlanta for a date. Mother fretted about the "wild" life of the university town, never knowing how little she had to worry about. Other than my parents' welfare, my main concern was scraping up enough money to make it through the first year.

I joined a fraternity, then wished I hadn't because it took up so much time. An opportunity to sell tailor-made shirts turned out to be my salvation. My best customers were the oversized football players, and the money I made from selling those shirts filled most of the gaps. Whenever he had money, Daddy deposited small sums in my checking account and sent me the deposit slips: $14, $11, or $7, whatever he'd taken in that day. I never knew from one day to the next when I'd wind up stony broke. I understood what Anne had gone through when she was at the University of Alabama, except that she hadn't had a job.

At Thanksgiving I got a ride home, happy for the break but dreading what I might find. No sooner had I set my suitcase down in my room than I noticed that my custom-made wooden bed had been severely broken in many places, then repaired. It was as if somebody had taken a crowbar or a baseball bat to it.

Mother was standing right there when I spotted it.

"Your daddy tore it apart in one of his rages," she said.

"My God, Mother, why in the world?"

She shrugged. "Who knows why he has those episodes?"

That was what we came to call them—his episodes. On a subsequent visit I found the same thing had happened to a chair in my room. Later two rocking chairs in our living room suffered the same fate. But the worst shock was the time I came home to find Mother's face battered and bruised. Daddy had done it, she said.

That was the last straw. "You have to leave him, Mother. You can't go on living like this."

"That's easy for you to say. I have nowhere to go, no money to live on except for my teaching job."

"Go back to Americus," I said, "and live with some of your relatives."

"I'd be too ashamed. Maybe at some point he'll get better, and until he does I just have to put up with it."

I didn't know it at the time, but Anne would tell me later that as far back as 1951, before Mother's father died, she had spoken to him about leaving Daddy because of his addiction. My grandfather refused to help, telling her she would have to handle her problems on her own. With no more family support than that, it was no wonder she had such a difficult and sometimes abrasive personality.

No matter how awful his mistreatment of her made me feel, I saw nothing to do but try to finish school and prepare myself for a career. Maybe then I could help her find a way out.

I WAS A COLLEGE JUNIOR when Daddy decided that since his Blakely practice showed no signs of improvement, he should relocate. He chose the tiny community of Morven, about a hundred miles away. When he left, Mother managed to buy a second car. Juanita went over to Morven once to help him but told him she couldn't keep working for him, because her family needed her at home. Doggedly, Daddy kept trying to make it work, while Mother stayed in Blakely to keep on with her piano lessons and hold down her school job. I knew she was relieved to have Daddy out of the house.

Occasionally she let me have her car for a while, which meant I could see Daphner. I happened to have it in Athens that winter when Mother called me in the dorm, after midnight.

"Son, please come home right away! Your daddy just called from Morven, wild as anything. He says he's on his way home to kill me, then kill himself."

"My God, Mother, I'm two hundred and fifty miles away. It'll take me five hours to get there."

"I know, but there's nobody to help me. I'm terrified. When he gets like this there's no telling what he'll do. Start right now, son, please! Just come!"

I closed my eyes. There was no escape. "All right. You lock yourself in the house, and when he gets there, don't dare let him in. I'll be there as soon as I can."

When I went back to the room and started packing a few things to leave, my roommate roused.

"Where d'you think you're going? In case you hadn't noticed, it's the middle of the night."

"There's an emergency at home." That was all I would say. Who'd want to admit that his dad was threatening to murder his mom? Taut as a banjo string, I drove through subfreezing temperatures on those black two-lane roads for hours. Dawn was breaking when I pulled in our drive, relieved to see that Daddy's car wasn't there. Mother, who had sat up all night, unlocked the door when she saw me get out of the car.

"Thank God you're here. Come in and I'll fix you something to eat."

"Never mind about that." I was looking around. "Where is he?"

"Heaven knows. He never came."

I made a couple of phone calls. Nobody knew anything, but after a few hours Daddy finally showed up, angry but not deranged. He'd run out of gas in an isolated spot and waited for hours before somebody happened across him and took him to get some gas.

"I'm lucky I didn't freeze to death," he said. "What are you doing home?"

"I'm here to protect Mother. Why in the world did you tell her you were coming to kill her?"

He stared at me, bewildered. "I didn't tell her any such thing."

"Oh, yes, you did. You called her and told her you were coming to kill her, then kill yourself. Why else do you think I'm here? I drove all night from Athens to help her."

"Son, you must be mistaken. I'd never do such a thing." And he really believed what he was saying.

HE FINALLY GAVE UP on the Morven practice and came back to Blakely to live out his days. Daddy's innate optimism was so great that he actually tried one more run for the state senate, and while he lost by only a small margin, that race put an end to all attempts to return to political life. It struck me as ironic—as a convicted felon he couldn't vote, yet he could still run for the Georgia Senate. His days afterward were of a dreary sameness—sitting in the office watching television or seeing an occasional patient, rambling around the square to stop in the barber shop or the drugstore or the beer joint, chewing the fat with whoever came along.

He got in the habit of occasionally calling up my friend John Puckett, who was several years younger than I, to invite him out to eat oysters. The oyster bar was one of those places where Daddy felt good about himself, and teen-aged John, pleased that an admired older person would seek out his company, greatly enjoyed the outings. Today, sad to say, some might look askance at such an association; back then nobody gave it a thought. Daddy never lost his love for people, especially young people, and like me and many others he enjoyed John's originality and sense of good fun. John is gone now too, and I and many in Blakely miss him.

MEANWHILE MY LIFE was moving ahead. I signed up for Army ROTC at Athens and—thanks to that early marksmanship training at Daddy's hands—made the ROTC rifle team. That was the good news. The bad news was that Daphner and I broke up for good. It would be so long before I was through with medical school and all my training that I couldn't see asking her to wait, though I'm profoundly sorry now that I didn't. The possibility that we might have married haunts me, because she was a fine girl whom I truly loved.

When I applied to the Medical College in Augusta, Daddy got all fired up about my prospects. He never doubted I would come back to Blakely to practice and redeem the family fortunes; I wasn't so sure. I knew my poor high school grades would count against me, but I'd done pretty well in my college studies except for nearly failing French—and I couldn't see what speaking French had to do with being a doctor anyhow. Surely my B in organic chemistry made up for that one weakness.

Daddy asked the *Augusta Chronicle*'s Talmadgeite editor to use his influence on my behalf but concluded, after my application got turned down, that the man had used his influence the other way. Political animosities in Georgia, particularly those of the race-baiters, died hard. Whatever the reason for my rejection, I was sorely disappointed, and Daddy was heartsick. We did everything we could to alter the decision, to no avail.

In the end I applied to Emory for dental school, which turned out to be a good decision. Thereafter I did extremely well, yet in Daddy's eyes the letters D.D.S. after my name would never be as exalted as M.D.

When I took an anatomy course I figured I could stump Daddy on the name of this or that insignificant bone; I figured wrong. Despite the fact that he continued to suffer episodes of derangement, he never failed to come up with the precise name, immediately, and he performed just as well when it came to biochemistry. The mad scientists of the federal prison might have damaged his mind, but every detail of his medical-school knowledge persisted after thirty-five years.

When in the course of my pharmacology studies I spotted Harris Isbell listed as an author of many professional articles, I found it incredible that a man widely recognized as a medical authority and researcher could be so despicable as to have dosed human beings with dangerous, harmful drugs without their knowledge.

MUCH AS I HATED TO ACCEPT THE FACT, Daphner, the love of my life, was a lost cause. All during dental school I worked nights in a hospital lab and eventually started dating one of the lab technicians. Over time I came to see this young woman as a potential life partner, and we married as soon as I graduated. We moved to the Gulf Coast then, because I went straight into the Air Force, stationed at Eglin Air Force Base. No assignment could have suited me better, with fine beaches close by, mild winters, and my parents in Blakely, only 125 miles away.

We set up housekeeping and were able to have Mother and Daddy visit us often. On one of those visits, Daddy suffered his second heart attack. It was not severe, but my internist friend who looked after him told me his heart was compromised and we should expect more of the same. In those days cardiac rehabilitation wasn't sophisticated. Also, Daddy had never overcome his addiction to nicotine and caffeine, nor had he kept off the weight lost while he was in Kentucky.

Over the next several years so much focused effort and activity occupied me as I completed my service obligation and looked after my growing family that I had little time to spend with my parents. Now and then I picked up guarded remarks from Mother that let me know Daddy was drinking more than he should and continued to suffer occasional episodes. She seemed to be coping with him, although after a visit home Anne told me that Daddy talked so obsessively about his troubles he sounded like a broken record.

Once or twice some relative called Anne: "What in the world's going on down in Blakely?" Anne tried to minimize things, but it wasn't easy. A visitor might notice the broken furniture plus a big stain on the dining-room wall—the result, Mother said, of a rage in which he hurled a full bottle of milk. At another time when Anne asked about a defect in the bathroom baseboard, Mother said it was where Daddy claimed he'd planted a microphone. For some reason that seemed to Anne like the worst thing of all.

"Mother, what on earth for?"

"Just more of his old craziness, thinking he'd catch me in something."

By the time I left the Air Force, a blessing had arrived for Daddy in the person of young McCall Calhoun, M.D., a physician fresh out of training who came to Blakely to set up practice. Reared in nearby Arlington in a family with several country doctors, Mac had known Daddy all his life, and his family's admiration for him never faltered. "Doctor Wall was railroaded," Mac's grandfather firmly believed.

Mac knew Daddy to be an expert diagnostician with a world of medical know-how and experience, so right away he sought him out as a mentor and called him to consult on special cases. A larger hospital was then being built in Blakely, and once it opened Mac enlisted Daddy as his first assistant for surgical procedures and consultant on obstetrical cases.

This new association with a respectful young doctor was far and away the best thing that had happened to Daddy in years. While Mac may not have taken a son's place in Daddy's eyes, he was the next thing to it. He appreciated Daddy's sense of humor and was the first Blakely colleague with whom Daddy ever felt entirely at ease. Undoubtedly the closest friend of Daddy's last years, Mac treasures a stock of wonderful stories about their association. Like Bob Hall and numerous others, he declares that Daddy "brought modern medicine to that part of the country." Mac remembers him as "an elegant, portly gentleman, big as a bale of cotton, with a mind like a steel trap. He had a tremendous personality and sense of humor, never forgot all these ridiculous things people get themselves into, and he would tell about them to give everybody a laugh."

Mac's recollections make it clear that vestiges of the old charismatic, convivial W. H. Wall still persisted. I think Daddy must have found it a constant and terrific strain to conceal his mental vagaries from anyone outside the family. Only in the privacy of home could he let down his guard and give way to frustration and rage, which may in part explain why he put Mother through so much hell.

Because the Calhoun family was also progressive-minded when it came to government, Mac understood quite well that Daddy's problems in politics arose because, unlike the South Georgia rank and file, he couldn't stick the Talmadge faction. After so much animosity and humiliation,

W. H. Wall, M.D., circa 1960.

Daddy found Mac's political sympathies most welcome. Mac also shares my own family's belief that Sid Howell and Dr. Jack Standifer, abetted by Howell's daughter-in-law Jane, were the main orchestrators of Daddy's downfall. Over time Daddy confided to Mac what he'd gone through in Lexington. Mac even knew about the episodes, but he kept it all to himself, totally respecting Daddy's privacy.

A delightful story Mac tells concerns one of his patients who was trying to deliver her eighth baby and having a dickens of a time because it was facing the wrong way.

She kept telling Mac that she could have the baby if only he'd let her do what she wanted to do.

"Please, Doctor Calhoun, just let me get down on the floor. I've had seven others, and I know I can have it then."

Mac told her, "Listen here, Mary, I can't possibly let you do that. If you get an infection and die, and the baby dies too, why, your people will hang me!"

Mac's nurse said, "Why don't you call Doctor Wall, see what he says?"

Mac called. Daddy came, and once he sized up the situation, Mac told him the woman wanted to get down on the floor.

Daddy said, "Well, let her do it."

"You have to be joking."

"No, I'm not. Go on and let her get down on the floor. They've been having babies for two thousand years without your help, and she's telling you something she feels like she needs to do."

So, reluctantly, Mac got the nurse to help spread a sterile sheet on the floor, and when the woman squatted, Mac got right down with her—"just like a mechanic under a car," he recalls. So there they were, the groaning, squatting woman, and Mac stretched out on the sheet alert for any progress. She had just about three hard pains, and lo and behold, a healthy baby slithered out.

Daddy leaned over to peer down. "Do I hear a baby crying?"

"Hell, yes, you hear a baby crying!" Mac said. And that baby was just fine.

Afterward Daddy just laughed and laughed. He told Mac, "You know, sometimes the patient knows more than the doctor. That woman's already had seven children, and do you know why she needed to get down on the floor?"

"No, I don't," Mac said.

Daddy told him, "Because God Almighty was telling her to do it. She knew that if she got on the floor, the head would come past her pelvic bone, and she'd deliver that baby."

Mac says that after that experience, any time he had an obstetrical patient who wanted to get down on the floor he told her to go right ahead. He claims he never stretched out like a mechanic again, just caught the baby before it hit the floor. And it always turned out all right.

DADDY'S EPISODES gradually lessened in frequency, though they left him a shadow of his old self. He often remained in his bedroom till midmorning unless he had to be up and out of the house on business of some kind, not necessarily asleep, sometimes reading the paper, sometimes just sitting on the side of his bed. When Mother thought he'd been idle long enough, she'd start nagging him to get up. Finally, in the late morning, he'd get up and dress.

After all, he had very little reason to get up, for compared to the past, his practice was virtually a phantom one. Over the six years of its existence under that name, Wall Hospital had served 1,857 patients, seen 192 births, and recorded forty-two deaths, not to mention the hundreds of patients he'd seen and babies he'd delivered in the previous fourteen years. The supreme self-confidence that had allowed him to build the hospital, perform major surgery, deliver hundreds of babies, and maintain the pre-eminent medical practice of the area was gone. It was a hard come-down.

In Early County, something else was gone as well: people. In the 1930s when Daddy came to town the county's population had been at an all-time high of about eighteen thousand, yet by 1960 the total was down to thirteen thousand, a much smaller population to draw from.

With both my parents nearing old age and money still tight, Daddy was thankful for the few patients who did come and did his best for them as he always had. As for Mother, who had begun her public-school career late in life, she had no choice but to continue until she accumulated enough service to qualify for retirement benefits. All through those years she was continually under strain and concerned about money, while Daddy never mentioned the word.

Anne and her family moved to Tallahassee, and on Sunday afternoons Mother and Daddy often drove down to see them. Their drives around northern Florida usually ended with Daddy stopping somewhere to buy beer to carry home, because on Sundays all the beer joints in Blakely were closed. I think E. B. suspected the beer was the primary purpose of the trip, and during those final years Daddy often drank too much.

ALREADY A HUSBAND, in 1964 I added the role of father when our first child, a son, was born. The following year I began a residency in maxillofacial surgery at Jackson Memorial Hospital in Miami, Florida, where

W. H. Wall, Sr., with grandchildren Cathy Williams and
W. H. Wall, III, circa 1965.

Mother and Daddy visited us once, to be followed by a second year of
residency in Atlanta back at Emory. We had a second baby, a little girl,
then in December of 1966 Daddy had to undergo an endarterectomy.
His surgeon and protégé, Dr. Milton Bryant, told me afterward that
although he had taken care of the immediate problem, x-ray studies
revealed an inoperable blockage at the base of Daddy's skull that was
bound to cause further trouble.

In July of the next year I was back in Florida for my final year of
residency at Duval Medical Center. Our third child and second son had

just been born, and Mother and Daddy planned to come to Jacksonville to see him. I was in the operating room doing a case with the senior plastic-surgery resident and Dr. Hehn, chairman of my department, when Dr. Hehn was called to the phone. In a few minutes he came back and told us to finish up, that he needed to see me as soon as we were done. It was most unusual for him to leave before the completion of any procedure. When we finished he took me aside.

"Henry," he said, "they want you to call Dr. Patterson in Cuthbert."

I knew what it was, even before I made the call. After one ring Dr. Patterson's wife answered. "I'm afraid it's not good news, Henry. Your father had a massive stroke today in his office. Juanita rode in the ambulance with him, and he died before they could get here. Your mother came up as soon as she heard, but he was already gone. I want you to know how very sorry we are. We thought the world of Doctor Wall."

Of course I left for home right away, regretting sorely that Daddy hadn't lived to see our baby boy or even learn his name. After I got to Blakely, Mother supplied the rest of the facts. At the moment of his attack Juanita had been in the front office, Daddy in his private office examining a man for an insurance physical. He had already signed the form, Juanita said, but hadn't completed filling it out. He seemed to know that his signature was the most important thing. Then all at once he cried out, "Oh, Juanita, help me, please! I'm so sick!"

Juanita went to him right away and when she saw him slumped over the examining table called for the ambulance. She knew Dr. Holland's hospital was out of the question; they would have to go to Cuthbert. Before they left she tried to reach Mother but couldn't locate her. She started giving him oxygen as they waited, and when the ambulance came, she went along so she could continue the oxygen on the way.

When they passed through the square she saw Mother on the street but couldn't get her attention. Daddy never spoke again. The driver covered the thirty miles at top speed, Juanita holding the oxygen mask to Daddy's face the whole way, but before they got there she saw that he was gone. It was over quickly, the way he would have wanted.

MOTHER, embittered by what she felt was a lack of support from her faith community, refused to hold the funeral at the Methodist Church, choosing a local funeral home instead. The place was far too small; the crowd spilled over to the porch and into the parking lot. At this service Mother made little effort to conceal her resentment, and we left immediately afterward for Ellaville, where Daddy was laid to rest with generations of his forebears. Very few people made the effort to go with us on to Ellaville, and that handful of people gathered in the family cemetery to bury a big man was one of the saddest assemblages I'd ever seen.

Daddy had left his country home with soaring hopes, distinguished himself through long and arduous training, then in a spirit of altruism settled in Early County to enjoy two unstinting decades of healing and service before calamity struck. He had exercised his training and talents not just for his own town and region but for the state of Georgia, only to be brought down not only by his addiction but, more importantly, by the jealous self-interest of a local doctor and a brutal sheriff's addiction to power.

It was finally all over. While Mother had apparently resigned herself long ago to life in the shadows, I'd never completely given up hope that he would regain the fullness of his natural joy in life, again rise to eminence in his town and his state, and reap the rewards he so well deserved.

No good man was ever more victimized. Now every chance for restoration had been swept away.

OVER THE YEARS after Daddy's death our long-drawn-out silent nightmare lay like a heavy weight on my heart. I couldn't talk about it, because I didn't trust others to understand—I was simply burdened with embarrassment and shame at so much of what had happened. Mother refused to discuss any of it; she wanted it swept under the rug and forgotten. Anne resisted the memories because her heart was secretly as sore as mine.

We didn't know it, but throughout our ordeal and for years afterward, all of us behaved like the typical family of an alcoholic or addict. We avoided the issue. We didn't name it—addiction, compounded by Isbell's heinous assault in Lexington. We did everything in our power to keep Daddy's secret from the outside world. We even withheld information from one another. Mother never spoke publicly about the facts and always minimized and rationalized Daddy's drug use, blaming the heavy pressures under which he labored.

Many years passed before I began dredging up memories and doing research for this book, decades before Anne and I began to talk to each other about what had been the most malignant influence of our lives. Once we did begin to open up, we learned that each of us had harbored startling secrets the other had never known. It was to become a remarkable journey of discovery.

For years after Daddy's death I was an extremely busy man. I moved to Atlanta to establish an oral surgery practice and accepted an appointment as associate clinical professor at Emory, where I had trained. The birth of our fourth child, a second daughter, rounded out our complement of two boys and two girls. My interest in biotechnical applications led me to obtain a dozen patents for my own devices and establish a company to manufacture and market them. The demands of my growing practice, my business, and my burgeoning family were so heavy that I had little time for anything else.

As for Anne, while E. B. went on to pursue further education, she too completed her bachelor's degree and then her master's. None of this was good enough for Mother, who badgered Anne about going on for a Ph.D. And all this time, whenever Daddy's name was mentioned, Anne broke down in tears. E. B. couldn't understand it and questioned her repeatedly about it.

Finally, about 1983, Anne went to a psychologist for counseling but took care never to mention the fact to Mother, who viewed seeking that kind of help as a disgrace. She later saw several counselors, but it was two years before she obtained insurance through her state job to assist with the expense.

Over a series of visits with a new therapist, the core issue soon came into focus. This wise professional recognized that Anne was continually re-experiencing a deep grief and told her frankly that she might never entirely overcome it. As this new therapist helped her to learn to express her feelings and discuss them openly, Anne kept going to school and studying harder and harder in an attempt to overcome the effects of our terrible ordeal.

After she completed her last degree in education, E. B. surprised her. "Now I want you to study law," he said. "I think you'll make an excellent lawyer."

Although Anne recognized that he might be on to something, she demurred. "Thanks for the compliment, but I could never do it—my family suffered too much at the hands of the legal profession."

Mother continued to harass her about getting yet another degree until finally Anne told her, "Look, Mother, I have no desire to go for a doctorate. I've already earned excellent degrees, and my family had to sacrifice enough while I was concentrating on my studies. I don't plan to study any more." For Anne that was a big breakthrough—standing up to Mother. What Anne did or didn't do in the academic line never seemed to upset Daddy. Both Anne and I always felt much closer to Daddy than to Mother, because he seemed to understand everyone and everything.

Yet the grief of his multiple tragedies was then almost unbearable for both of us, and in Anne's case it has never entirely healed. My own healing has begun, through opening up to my collaborator on this book about the traumas of the past, but I'm sure I still have a long way to go.

Chapter 10

"We do not target American citizens . . . The nation must to a
degree take it on faith that we who lead the CIA are honorable
men, devoted to the nation's service."

— RICHARD HELMS, former CIA director

In March of 1979 the revelation came. After Times Books published
journalist John Marks's nonfiction opus *The Search for the Manchurian
Candidate*, a horrifying exposé of a Central Intelligence Agency (CIA)
program known as MKULTRA that focused on attempts to find an effective mind-control or "truth" drug, *The Atlanta Journal-Constitution*
featured a series of six articles detailing the book's content. By the time I
read the second page of the second installment I knew exactly what had
happened to my dad. Stunned, I read it again slowly to be quite sure.

As Marks reported, the linchpin of the MKULTRA program was
the compound d-lysergic acid diethylamide, or LSD. I had heard plenty
about this hallucinogen through the 1960s headline-grabbing antics of
Timothy Leary, Ken Kesey, Allen Ginsberg, and other derangement
devotees. Sought by some as a mind-expander, at times the LSD experience or "acid trip" plunged other users into terrifying sensations and led
to ghastly flashbacks that might persist for years.

More to the point as far as Daddy was concerned, its bad effects were
said to be even greater for a person given the drug in "circumstances not
conducive to pleasant feelings"—as when you were given it by someone
you despised, when colleagues had turned against you, when you were in
prison, when you were struggling to overcome a narcotic habit on your
own while everything you'd built up for years was being auctioned off
on the courthouse square. Given the hallucinogen in such a situation,

anyone might conclude that the world was plotting against him—no doubt the message Isbell had tried to implant. And I already knew from my pharmacological studies how far-reaching could be the aftereffects of a bad LSD trip, unique to this particular drug.

At long last I had the logical explanation of the sudden onset of Daddy's terror of being driven insane, of the mental derangement that persisted as paranoia and "episodes" for years after his release. All of the elements matched up.

And among the various names of scientists mentioned in the article one simply leapt off the page: "Dr. Harris Isbell, director of the Addiction Research Center at the huge federal drug hospital in Lexington, Kentucky." A hospital they might call it, but it was a prison for narcotics offenders, with the nationally acclaimed Isbell heading the center's program. The very man whom Daddy so despised for his cavalier attitude toward drug-dependent patients in his charge, the enthusiastic dispenser of potions who enticed prisoner-addicts to volunteer for his experiments.

Among Isbell's reports of his chemical experiments, he boasted, according to Marks, of having kept seven men on LSD for seventy-seven straight days. And in cases where the response was not all that he hoped for, he doubled, tripled, even quadrupled the dose, noting that some of the subjects seemed to fear the doctors. My God, who wouldn't have feared them? Such torment hardly bears imagining.

To put it plainly, what Harris Isbell did to my father was to assault him with a poison that permanently damaged his brain. In this day of effective alcohol and drug rehabilitation programs, it's unthinkable that American citizens' taxes paid this man to destroy his hostages' minds and lives.

Can you imagine yourself a respectable, middle-aged, recently prominent, heretofore sane, professional man, being told god knows what as the walls undulate around you, the drab hospital room glows with psychedelic light, the air hums with unearthly vibrations, and the faces of those around you constantly shift from human to animal to gargoyles and back to human again? It's scarcely imaginable, but that was what happened to Daddy.

As he shuddered through these weird visual and auditory sensations, Daddy would often have felt nauseated, perspired profusely, and had "goose-bump" skin and a racing heart. His blood sugar would shoot up—bad news for a diabetic—and at times he would feel himself grow huge, then imagine he had shrunk to the size of his own thumb. No wonder he phoned Mother in a panic to report they were giving him something to make him lose his mind.

As the long days and nights dragged on, his fears and depression surely mounted. He told us little about it, but relatively normal periods probably alternated with acute panic reactions and repeated psychotic episodes— what we know today as "flashbacks." Daddy had never heard of LSD and knew nothing about such experiences, let alone sought them.

Expecting to be paroled after four and a half months at most, he was kept in Lexington for eight, incarcerated a total of nine if you include his month in Georgia jails, with the final five of those months made nightmarish by LSD.

Further imagine, if you will, the insanity of making a man in the throes of such derangements responsible for another, more gravely ill person's care. Surely the poor old black addict from Chicago with advanced TB deserved better. I don't doubt for a minute that Daddy looked after him as best he could, but who could remain a balanced, thoroughly vigilant nurse in the grip of such mental torment?

It is a testament to the basically sound fabric of my father's mind and constitution that he survived without taking his own life or that of any other.

The CIA's ill-conceived covert Cold War scheme to find a mind-control drug for use on hostile leaders had caught my patriot father in its hateful web, as much a prisoner of war as if he were locked in a Communist prison. For thirteen years afterward he would strive manfully to break free, but for all practical purposes his life was ruined.

Once I grasped that much, I believed I understood why Daddy had been kept on in Lexington beyond the usual "cure" period referred to in his letters. The additional time was to allow Isbell to observe and record his behavior following the drug assault. Even when he was finally sent home, having received no treatment of any sort for his drug dependence, Isbell made no provision whatever for psychiatric or medical follow-up. I found it heinous beyond belief that this violated man, still prey to paranoid flashbacks, was simply turned loose to his bewildered family and whatever fate might overtake him.

On the one occasion when Isbell did invite Daddy to volunteer for his drug tests, Daddy refused outright. He never knew what persuaded his fellow inmates to sign up, but from Marks I learned the answer. Those who volunteered either got time off from their sentences or else were rewarded with the purest doses of their preferred drug—generally heroin or morphine. They were addicts, after all, and most chose their reward of choice. How much easier it was to get high in the safety of a clean hospital room where three meals a day were provided, as opposed to the dangerous daily struggle to cop a fix on the street. It's not surprising that as word got out via the addicts' grapevine, recidivism at Lexington approached ninety percent.

Once I learned of the reward system, it also seemed obvious that the politically astute Isbell would never have risked offering Daddy, a prominent narcotic-addicted physician sent there to break free of his drug, a reward in the form of that same narcotic. Had he presented Daddy with such an outrageous offer, Daddy would have done all in his power to blow the whistle on the man—fruitlessly, of course, in view of the CIA's shield of secrecy. Isbell probably used that single offer to test the waters with Daddy, then backed off from further attempts at persuasion.

When Daddy turned him down, Isbell must then have ordered surreptitious dosing with the hallucinogen. How was it done? Daddy always thought it was in his food or something given him to drink. The easiest way might have been a tiny speck of LSD in the water pitcher beside Daddy's bed. Odorless, colorless, and tasteless, the chemical was undetectable other than by the mental derangement it caused.

God knows how many others at Lexington were also Isbell's guinea pigs. To Daddy's credit—and thanks to his resourcefulness—he caught on quickly enough to take himself out of the "experiment" by refusing all food and drink except for water and canned soup. But he still drank water, so though his dosage might have been reduced, he was probably still getting LSD.

And Isbell was only one of numerous scientists at prestigious institutions who accepted CIA grants to run LSD experiments on human subjects. Many students at various colleges and universities were paid to participate. The first medical centers to receive grants were Boston Psychopathic Hospital (later renamed Massachusetts Mental Health Center), New York's Mt. Sinai and Columbia hospitals, the University of Illinois Medical School, Isbell's own center at Lexington operating under the respectable cover of the Navy and National Institutes of Mental Health (NIMH), and the universities of Oklahoma and Rochester.

While I knew I had found the answer to questions we had agonized over for so many years, I still found it hard to take in all that I had read. Could an agency of my own U.S. government truly have authorized and funded such reprehensible abuse of a loyal citizen and public servant, a sick man whose only crime was becoming dependent upon a painkiller his doctors had prescribed? Undoubtedly there was much more to be learned, but for the first installment this was more than enough.

I WENT BACK to read the first of the newspaper installments, pounced on the ones that followed day by day, and began to put all the known facts into place. Apparently the first U.S. concerns about behavior and mind control had arisen during the 1940s in the wartime Office of Strategic Services (OSS) created for intelligence work, about the same time that Germany's SS and Gestapo doctors were experimenting on Dachau prisoners with mescaline, another hallucinogen. In the U.S. the OSS set up its own "truth drug" committee and tested mescaline, barbiturates, and scopolamine before settling on a concentrated extract of marijuana as their best hope.

With an eye to persuading the Mafia to help protect New York's harbor from enemy infiltrators and support the invasion of Sicily, an OSS captain named George White first used the doped cigarettes to loosen up a New York gangster. With that first modest success the U.S. government's mind-control quest was underway.

By 1946, revelations about atrocities performed by Nazi doctors impelled the Nuremberg war-crimes judges to draw up an international standard for scientific research that became known as the Nuremberg Code. It stated that no persons could be experimented on without their full voluntary consent, that all experiments should add to the good of society, and that no experiments could risk death or serious injury unless the researchers themselves served as test subjects.

The following year brought sufficiently great concerns about the aims of Communist regimes that the U.S. Congress passed the National Security Act. Under one of its provisions the wartime OSS was succeeded by a new organization, the CIA. At the time, former President Herbert Hoover expressed sentiments fairly typical of the national outlook:

> . . . We are facing an implacable enemy whose avowed object is world domination by whatever means and at whatever cost. There are no rules in such a game. Hitherto acceptable longstanding American concepts of "fair play" must be reconsidered. We must . . . learn to subvert, sabotage, and destroy our enemies by more clever, sophisticated, and more effective methods than those used against us.

Many of the CIA's personnel were OSS holdovers, and while they could not quite sink to the chilling inhumanity of the Nazi doctors, the CIA took up the mind-control work. Upright Mr. Hoover surely had no inkling of the lengths to which the embryo Agency would go, once notions of fair play fell away. The CIA's men would go on to experiment, as Marks observed, "with dangerous and unknown techniques on people who had no idea what was happening . . . [They] systematically violated the free will and mental dignity of their subjects and . . . chose to victimize . . . groups of people whose existence they considered . . . less worthy than their own."

The Nazis had abused Jews, gypsies, and prisoners; the CIA experimenters would prey on "mental patients, prostitutes, foreigners, drug addicts, and prisoners, often from minority ethnic groups" (most of the Lexington subjects were black). Mentally defective persons by the very nature of their affliction could never have given fully informed consent, yet they too became subjects for some of the mind-control tests. In the end the CIA zanies would violate every precept of the Nuremberg Code.

THE FIRST WIDESPREAD public concerns about MKULTRA had been raised by the 1975 Rockefeller Commission's hearings, with more information coming to light through congressional hearings led by Senators Frank Church and Edward Kennedy. Their findings prompted *The New York Times* to publish a front-page article headlined "Private Institutions Used in C.I.A. Effort to Control Behavior." Other national magazines—*Time,* for one—ran similar pieces, but if I ever saw any of those articles, they failed to stick in my mind. Not until I read the 1979 Atlanta series summarizing Marks's book did I grasp the full horror of what had gone on.

In its early years the CIA was such a small, clubby, shadowy organization that few Americans even knew existed, but alarms about mind control—or brainwashing—arose within its close-knit ranks in response to the glassy-eyed 1949 confession of Jósef Cardinal Mindszenty at his Budapest treason trial. Convinced with Hoover that the Communists were dead-set on world domination, the CIA honchos believed the Russians were using methods of mind control to further that aim. Determined to be prepared to fight fire with fire, the Agency accelerated its mind-control movement, with disastrous results for thousands of American citizens and ultimately, I believe, for American society as a whole.

In that same year of 1949 Dr. Robert Hyde of Boston became the first known American LSD tripper. It made him paranoid for a time, yet he went on to become a consultant to the CIA. After Dr. Hyde's maiden hallucinogenic voyage, little was known about the mind-blowing drug when a rumor arose claiming that its sole manufacturer, the Swiss pharmaceutical concern Sandoz, had sold the Russians fifty million doses of LSD. Blind to the rumor's absurdity and panicked at the thought of such a weapon in Communist hands, the CIA began work on its own plans for the chemical, as the U.S. Army was already doing.

By 1950, CIA teams were running secret chemical tests on North Korean prisoners of war hoping to achieve mind control, amnesia, or both. The year that followed was a crucial one for the mind and behavior-control impetus. Allen Dulles, who had graduated from spying for the OSS to become the CIA's director, vividly recalled a wartime meeting with Dr. Albert Hofmann, the Sandoz chemist who discovered LSD. Hofmann told Dulles that after inadvertently dosing himself with the drug he became so terrified that he "would have confessed to anything." On the basis of that startling admission, Dulles authorized his CIA people to cooperate with U.S. military intelligence and British and Canadian teams in a behavior-control program first called PROJECT BLUEBIRD, later renamed PROJECT ARTICHOKE.

Responsibility for recruiting medical scientists for ARTICHOKE went to the Agency's Technical Services Staff (TSS), with instructions to enlist only those experimenters with no moral or ethical scruples about engaging in possibly lethal work. Around this same time the CIA also considered electroshock experiments and neurosurgical techniques for behavior control.

Besides concentrated marijuana, drugs used in the CIA and Army experiments included cocaine, heroin, PCP, amyl nitrate, psilocybin, hallucinogenic mushrooms, barbiturates, nitrous oxide, speed, alcohol, morphine, ether, benzedrine, mescaline, and a host of others. But LSD quickly became the favorite, as it had the most powerful effects. Subjects who took it might become extremely anxious, lose contact with reality, and suffer severe mental confusion. They hallucinated and often became paranoid, experiencing acute distortions of time, place, and body image. The experimenters never knew what their subjects' mood might be—anything from panic to bliss. The drug produced mental states similar to those known to occur in schizophrenia: intense color perceptions, depersonalization, psychic disorganization, and disintegration. The paramount effect was a breakdown in a subject's character defenses for handling anxiety—bad stuff indeed, and just the kind of thing the CIA was looking for.

In April of 1953, as Daddy's modest Blakely enterprises collapsed, Allen Dulles and his former OSS colleague and now henchman Richard Helms put Helms' protégé, a clubfooted Ph.D. chemist and former

Young Socialist from Caltech named Sidney Gottlieb, in charge of AR-TICHOKE, rechristened MKULTRA, with the specific aim of exploring "covert use of biological and chemical and radiological materials." The initial MKULTRA budget was three hundred thousand dollars, by no means small for the time. Eager to see for himself what LSD could do, Gottlieb focused on it, and to his victims' eternal loss, MKULTRA was off and running.

In spite of warnings that LSD was known to produce insanity that could last "for periods of eight to eighteen hours and possibly for longer," the Agency's medical office issued a mind-boggling recommendation: all CIA personnel should be given LSD, across the board. Many agents took it, including the MKULTRA gang. That fact alone should have raised red flags. How many of them were made crazy themselves? After who knows how many acid trips, would you or I trust ourselves to make wise decisions?

Elated with these beginnings in spite of a few observed "bad trips," Gottlieb, who would eventually *admit to two hundred LSD trips of his own,* then decided to test his favorite mind-bender on unsuspecting persons in other countries and made multiple trips abroad with a stash of LSD for the purpose. He knew his superiors approved the secret dosing of unwitting people, contending that if a subject knew what he would be given and when, it would affect his response and skew the test.

While Gottlieb and his gang continued their freelance chemical capers, they were beginning to want reputable scientific research to back up their theories. Scientists at NIMH were also interested in learning more about LSD. If any large-scale testing of the drug was to be done, however, money must be found to pay for it. Gottlieb quickly rose to the challenge. From their vast CIA treasure chest he and his MKULTRA cohort arranged to channel enormous sums of Agency money to select consultants at well-known medical or educational institutions, in the guise of grants from two foundations—the Geschickter Fund for Medical Research and the Josiah Macy, Jr., Foundation. A third faked-up conduit, the Society for the Investigation of Human Ecology, would later come into play.

Although the CIA origins of the money were not made public,

recipients were well aware of its true source, because Gottlieb and his underlings often visited the project sites, and the researchers reported directly to them. The Agency cloaked the project in utmost secrecy, knowing very well what a hue and cry would erupt if the American public caught wind of such nefarious goings-on. Secrecy about CIA involvement was definitely preserved at Lexington. Hungry for status and acclaim, the power-drunk Dr. Isbell enhanced his own professional standing by publishing articles about his activities, though taking care never to state that his subjects were federal prisoners.

Irrefutable evidence that Gottlieb understood the need for secrecy was the early agreement he made with his mentor Helms to keep no records of MKULTRA activities. Before these co-conspirators retired two decades later, they would make strenuous efforts to destroy what few incriminating files did exist. Had they not missed some one hundred thirty boxes, we would never know the havoc they wrought.

Just after Daddy was transported to Lexington, MKULTRA suffered what should have been a fatal setback, barely concealed by the Agency's clumsy efforts at secrecy. A Ph.D. biochemist named Frank Olson was one of the scientists assigned to the Army Chemical Corps' Special Operations Division (SOD) at Fort Detrick, Maryland, working on diseases and toxins that ranged from instantly lethal chemicals to bacteria capable of disabling without killing the targeted person. An anthrax specialist, Olson was actually on the CIA's payroll, and he and his boss, Lt. Col. Vincent Ruwet, were included in a three-day working SOD-CIA retreat at an isolated lodge in western Maryland.

Gottlieb was also present, and in the course of their stay undertook to try out his pet hallucinogen on the unsuspecting group. He laced a bottle of Cointreau with LSD and offered it to the others after the evening meal. When all but two of those present had swallowed their drinks, he told them what he had done—or so he would later claim.

Calamity was the result. While the other four Cointreau trippers became giggly and uninhibited, Olson went completely around the bend. Unable to make sense of what was going on, he couldn't understand why the others were laughing and believed he was the butt of their jokes. Persistently agitated the next morning, he returned home in what his wife called a highly atypical state and told her he had been ridiculed by his colleagues for a dreadful mistake but refused to give details. The following day, still deeply disturbed, he reported to work intent on resigning but was persuaded by Ruwet to wait. When his agitation continued and Ruwet called on the CIA for advice, the decision was made to get Olson to New York to see Dr. Harold Abramson, one of the MKULTRA grant recipients who believed, eccentrically, in alcohol as a useful antidote for a bad acid trip. (Abramson had first come to Gottlieb's attention when he proposed giving mentally sound patients LSD without their knowledge for "psychotherapeutic purposes.")

In the role of Olson's minders, Ruwet and Robert Lashbrook, another CIA man, went along. They made no objections when Dr. Abramson left Olson in the hotel room with a bottle of bourbon and a quantity of barbiturate pills—a combination which, taken in a large enough quantity, can be fatal. The night before Olson was to return to his family for Thanksgiving, he went out of the hotel in a delusional state to wander the streets. He threw away his wallet, tore up all his currency, believing it to be secret orders of some sort, and discarded his government identification. With daylight he, Ruwet, and Lashbrook took a plane back to Washington, but once there Olson refused to see his family for fear he might turn violent. The situation was desperate. Ruwet left to allay the Olson family's concerns, while Lashbrook returned to New York with their pitiably disturbed charge.

When Dr. Abramson saw the psychotic Olson and realized the problem was beyond his competence, he arranged for Olson to enter a Maryland sanitarium the next day, one that was considered secure by the CIA. After Lashbrook checked the two of them into a New York hotel room for the night, Olson phoned his wife to tell her he was better. Lashbrook would later report going to sleep only to awaken in the wee hours just in time to see Olson tear across their tenth-floor room at a run, then crash headlong through the drawn blinds and closed window. The tormented scientist plummeted to the sidewalk below and was found there by the hotel's night manager, barely alive and mumbling incoherently. An ambulance was called, but he died before anyone could learn who he was or why he'd fallen.

After an in-house inquiry at the CIA, Lashbrook left the Agency, while Gottlieb—who was taken to task only mildly—said that the drug had no serious side effects and that Olson's death was just one of the risks of scientific experiments. He was allowed to continue his MKULTRA activities for another nineteen years.

The Agency did its best to convince the Olson family that its despondent breadwinner had committed suicide. Ruwet always kept in touch with the family, and the CIA saw to it that Mrs. Olson received her husband's government pension. But she was unable to forget that in the months before he died, something connected with his work had troubled her husband profoundly, and she refused to believe he would intentionally abandon her or his three children. For a time, that was as far as the story went.

TWO DECADES LATER, after James Schlesinger was named head of the CIA in 1973, he issued orders that all CIA employees were to inform him of any "improper or illegal acts" the Agency might have carried out. He must have had no idea how much damning information would pour in. While Nixon fought the Watergate scandal, Schlesinger fielded a spate of reports going back as far as the North Korean and Vietnam conflicts, including the very first schemes of Gottlieb and his loose-cannon squad. In the purge that followed Schlesinger fired at least two hundred fifty CIA employees before Nixon extricated him from the morass by appointing him Secretary of Defense. Gottlieb and Helms stayed on.

Schlesinger's CIA successor, William Colby, was another former OSS man, well aware he had inherited a colossal nightmare. To his credit, he stuck to the job through an unprecedented public outcry until his mysterious death while boating on a Maryland river.

In December of 1974, Seymour Hersh of *The New York Times* brought the Olson family's tragedy to public notice, implying that the CIA had run rampant for years. At that point President Ford named Vice-President Nelson Rockefeller head of a blue-ribbon panel to investigate the whole mess, including MKULTRA. When the Rockefeller Commission brought its full report back to Congress and the President, included were recommendations for future avoidance of such scandals. Among its findings, the Commission verified that twenty-two years previously an unnamed civilian unwittingly given LSD by the CIA had plunged from a New York hotel window to his death. The facts were too congruent for the Olsons to ignore. Pressed by Olson's daughter, Ruwet finally admitted what had happened, or at least gave her the CIA's doctored version of events.

Outraged, the Olson family went public and sued the U.S. government. They received a personal apology in 1976 from President Gerald Ford and a compensation award of seven hundred fifty thousand dollars from Congress on condition that they never speak publicly of the matter again. By this time Director Colby had revealed enough Agency secrets that Richard Helms was convicted of perjury and given a suspended jail term and a two thousand dollar fine, which his buddies paid because in CIA circles ratting on one's colleagues "simply wasn't done." After Colby's death George H. W. Bush replaced him to serve in the job for one year. Neither Gottlieb nor the CIA ever admitted any wrongdoing. But no matter how fervently the CIA spooks hoped they'd quashed their dirty little story, there was still more to come.

Forty years after Frank Olson's death, Harvard professor Michael Ignatieff, an international authority on human rights and former classmate of Olson's son Eric, took up the Olson case and in a *New York Times* piece raised many troubling questions about the official version of events. As Ignatieff reported, many years after the tragedy Eric Olson had gone to New York and visited the hotel room from which his father was said to have thrown himself to his death. Already suspicious of the official account, young Olson discovered that the room was too small to allow anyone to run at the window, the window sill too high and too obstructed for anyone to go over it with enough force to crash through a closed blind and window. Still in search of a credible explanation, Eric Olson, his brother, and his mother called on both Gottlieb and Lashbrook but got nothing out of either of them.

Frank Olson's passport indicated several trips to Europe in the sum-

mer of 1953, and according to Ignatieff's account, a British journalist
with good reason to know told Eric how during that summer Olson had
told a London psychiatrist he was deeply troubled by secret U.S.-British
experiments he had witnessed in Germany. The journalist's guess was
that Olson had seen some truth-serum and interrogation experiments
that ended in the death of one or more "captured Russian agents and
ex-Nazis." Furthermore, the CIA files turned over to the Olsons by Colby
supported Mrs. Olson's recollection of her husband's disturbed state of
mind that summer and fall, when Agency personnel had raised official
doubts about Frank Olson's security clearance.

After Dr. Olson's death his body had been embalmed, and the CIA
told the family the casket must be closed because of the body's broken-
up condition and many facial lacerations caused by window glass. Yet
in 1994 when Eric had his father's body exhumed he found it almost
perfectly preserved, with no facial lacerations. George Washington University forensic specialists who examined the remains found evidence of
a fist-sized blow to the dead man's left temple and concluded it could
only have occurred *before* his fall.

On the basis of all he had learned, Eric Olson was convinced that
rather than committing suicide, his father had been murdered by the
CIA—rendered defenseless by a knockout punch, possibly with the aid
of some drug, then thrown from that hotel window. After further investigations led him to believe that the CIA brought in contract killers to do
the job, he saw the scenario as a cover-up to keep the troubled scientist
from airing his deep anxieties about what the Agency was doing. Defini-
tive answers may never be known—suffice it to say that Gottlieb and
MKULTRA destroyed another useful life and forever wrecked another
family's peace.

BACK IN 1954, while the Olsons mourned their loss and Daddy was
released from prison, Eli Lilly & Co. in Indianapolis had succeeded in
synthesizing LSD "in tonnage amounts," giving the CIA a more than ample
supply for MKULTRA and future grant recipients. The Army and other
military services continued their own mind-control experimentation, with

cooperation from other U.S. government agencies including the Food and Drug Administration (FDA) and the Bureau of Narcotics.

After the Bay of Pigs debacle in Cuba, President Kennedy and his brother, Attorney General Robert Kennedy, had agreed that Allen Dulles must be replaced at the CIA. In 1961 John A. McCone was named to the position, while durable Richard Helms was put in charge of Clandestine Services and Gottlieb kept his job running MKULTRA. Strong objections about the program were raised two years later when, after some substantial digging, the inspector general McCone appointed, John Earman, strongly recommended that MKULTRA be shut down, declaring that many in the Agency viewed its work as "distasteful and unethical." When McCone put certain elements of the project on hold, Helms bombarded him with demands to continue the unwitting mind-control tests. Subsequent Agency-funded tests sucked a young professor named Timothy Leary into its web, and the rest of the LSD story, as they say, is history.

By 1966, when Helms was finally promoted to director of the CIA, Gottlieb knew he could breathe easy and go on with the business, as Gordon Thomas would declare in his CIA exposé *Journey Into Madness*, of "devising new and better ways to disorient and discredit, to maim and kill."

The world was already learning more than it wanted to know about LSD, as a cover story in *Life* reported: "A person can become permanently deranged through a single terrifying LSD experience." Yet another senate subcommittee was convened to address the growing LSD problem among the young, but Robert Kennedy, now a U.S. senator, objected to suggestions that all LSD experimentation be curtailed,. Amid rumors that his wife Ethel had undergone LSD therapy, which could explain her husband's resistance, he said, ". . . we have lost sight of the fact that [LSD] can be very, very helpful in our society if used properly."

It might have seemed by this time that much of the world had gone mad. The poet Allen Ginsberg was urging every American over the age of fourteen to drop LSD for "a mass emotional nervous breakdown." In response to the public uproar, Sandoz called in all the LSD it had supplied to U.S. researchers. But the FDA would not back down from its involvement in LSD research. Instead, it moved to set up a joint FDA-NIMH body known as the Psychomimetic Advisory Committee and put at least one of the CIA's grant-recipient foxes in charge of the henhouse when it named Harris Isbell to the new committee.

By 1968, possession of LSD had become a misdemeanor and sale of the drug a felony. Two years afterward it was listed as a Schedule I drug—a drug of abuse with no medical value. A Bureau of Narcotics pamphlet issued in 1969 stated as a matter of history that the CIA's dissemination of LSD through the scientific and intellectual community was responsible for the alarming popularity of the drug. Even though people all over the country and especially disaffected young people were resorting to it, the CIA continued to deny any suggestion that it had promoted a market for the drug. But if not the CIA or the Army, then who? The late John Lennon certainly gave credit to both.

Once other entrepreneurs learned how to produce LSD and moved it onto the black market beyond the CIA's and FDA's control, the psychedelic era was under way. As the Grateful Dead's tripping followers were to declare, it would be a long, strange journey indeed.

Elected president in 1972, Richard Nixon had removed Richard Helms from the CIA's ranks by appointing him ambassador to Iran and put Schlesinger in his place. But before Helms left and Gottlieb retired, they oversaw the purging of any file documents or tapes that might be useful in prosecutions against them or the Agency. With two such Machiavellian types gone, the air at Langley, Virginia, must have taken a remarkably fresher turn.

Chapter 11

"A free society's best defense against unethical behavior modification is public disclosure and awareness . . . The more vigilant we and our representatives are, the less chance we will be unwitting victims."

— JOHN MARKS, *The Search for the "Manchurian Candidate"*

Mother finally decided she had had enough of living in Blakely, a place with far too many painful memories for her. She had worked long enough to qualify for a teacher's pension and paid off every cent of the loan on the house. Now she told me she was moving to a nice retirement community in her hometown of Americus and wanted Anne and me to sell the Flowers Drive house as soon as she selected the pieces of furniture she wanted to take with her. I was relieved to see her settled where she would be happier and well looked after, but getting her moved and disposing of everything she and Daddy had accumulated over the years took a lot of time and energy. Through the lean and traumatic years their house had fallen into considerable disrepair; it was a good thing we didn't know that twelve years would pass before the place sold.

About that same time I became involved in a lawsuit, having to do with my biotechnical patents, which was a tremendous financial drain and took up far more time than I liked. And if all that weren't enough, my marriage had gone permanently sour. The problems between us were such that no amount of counseling would help, so for the children's sake, rather than deprive them of the security of a two-parent home, I turned a blind eye to one intolerable event after another and resolved to tough it out until our youngsters were grown. What would happen at that point I didn't think about and couldn't have said.

With the normal demands of a houseful of active, growing children and the abnormal one of an increasingly hostile wife, each new day brought such plentiful conflicts and challenges that I had little time to dwell on the troubles of the past.

Yet Marks's discoveries and revelations kept coming back to my mind. What Isbell and the other MKULTRA participants had done to American citizens was unconscionable. My father was only one of countless numbers of victims, and he at least had come out of it alive. How many others had committed suicide, or ended their days confined to mental hospitals once their brains were completely fried? Most of the guilty parties were still alive—they had to be called to account.

Eventually, I resumed my research. I discovered that *Time* had reported LSD experiments between 1955 and 1958 at Michigan's Ionia State Hospital, experiments similar to those in Lexington and also funded by the CIA. At Ionia, LSD and marijuana were tried out as "truth drugs" on criminal sexual psychopaths.

I learned that CIA-paid experimenters in Providence, Rhode Island, preyed on both staff and mental patients at Butler Memorial Hospital. Other experiments were organized by a Dr. Carl Pfeiffer at the New Jersey Reformatory in Bordentown. A pharmacologist, Pfeiffer had left the University of Illinois to join the faculty at Emory University, where I would later graduate in dentistry, running experiments at the Federal penitentiary in Atlanta. So if we had succeeded in getting Daddy transferred to Atlanta when he begged us to, we would only have put him into a new tormentor's hands.

A Scots-born naturalized America citizen, D. Ewen Cameron, carried out the most horrendous tortures of all at Allan Memorial Institute of Psychiatry in Montreal. Men, women, and even teenagers consigned for mostly minor problems to his sadistic care deteriorated into blithering idiots, for lack of a better term. A rapaciously ambitious man like Isbell, Cameron was considered one of the foremost North American physicians in his field. Professor of psychiatry at McGill University and psychiatrist-in-chief of Montreal's prestigious Royal Victoria Hospital as well as director of Allan Memorial, he would in time hold the presidencies of four psychiatric associations—American, Quebec, Canadian, and World, having been a founder of the latter. One of three North American psychiatrists to evaluate the Nazi prisoner Rudolph Hess at Nuremberg, he had published a paper about his Nuremberg experience. Like Isbell, he was named to the Psychomimetic Advisory Committee.

At Allan Memorial. Cameron plied his victims with mind-ravaging drugs, subjected them to unbelievably cruel sensory deprivation, and forced them to listen to endless taped hours of brainwashing—again, all in contravention of the Nuremberg Code, and funded by the CIA.

I LEARNED MORE about MKULTRA. At the 1977 Kennedy hearings, the CIA's then director, Admiral Stansfield Turner, summarized the extent of MKULTRA activities as reported in *Time:*

"149 projects for an undisclosed amount of money at eighty U.S. and Canadian universities, research foundations, hospitals, and prisons. At least thirty-nine projects involved human subjects, *often without their knowledge.*" [emphasis added] He estimated that as much as ten million dollars of taxpayers' money went for MKULTRA initiatives. Today when talk of billions and even trillions in government expenditures is common, ten million dollars may not seem exorbitant, but in 1977 it was a colossal amount.

Determined that the old nightmarish plots and projects never be repeated, Admiral Turner also reported that while MKULTRA experiments began winding down in 1964, some had continued all the way to 1973, which meant that for nineteen years after the permanent rewiring of my father's brain, untold legions of human guinea pigs endured these mad scientists' torments. As for psychiatric or medical follow-up, Turner admitted that no one knew the current whereabouts of the subjects or what aftereffects they might have suffered.

Well, I knew the whereabouts of one—William Henry Wall, M.D. After suffering the tortures of the damned for thirteen years, that particular hapless victim died a broken man at the age of sixty-four. If anyone were to speak for him, I would have to be the man.

As John Marks declared, if any ordinary academic or professional scientist had been discovered to hold his subjects prisoner, inject or dose them without their consent or knowledge with unnamed drugs, such a person would be charged with kidnapping or aggravated assault and undoubtedly disgraced in his profession. Yet because these acts were committed under the aegis of the CIA, the researchers evaded all legal and professional consequences.

Even after the Church and Kennedy hearings ended, except for Admiral Turner's disclosures, the CIA's brotherhood of silence was still in force. Because Senator Edward Kennedy had not briefed himself sufficiently to hammer out the hard challenges, his hearings did little to expand public knowledge about MKULTRA and the CIA's experiments. If it was true that his sister-in-law Ethel had submitted to LSD therapy as rumored, he may not have felt any more strongly than his brother Robert about the damage the hallucinogen could do. Marks did not complete his book until after the Kennedy hearings were over, and with still more boxes of MKULTRA files turning up, he found evidence to substantiate accusations of perjury against some CIA people who had testified, denying activities they were known to have participated in.

This mind-blowing research had burrowed into my soul at a difficult time. I was working hard to build my practice and biotechnical business, putting out large sums on patents and manufacturing, all for future security. My children were growing up, still in need of funds for education, while my marriage was miserable. I looked for the day when such obligations would be past and I would be free to take up the cause unencumbered.

I took the first tentative steps in October of 1985. I first wrote to the CIA and the State Department, asking for "information concerning compensation and awards paid to victims of government agency experiments with LSD." I stated that "these experiments took place from 1953 to 1960 and were conducted . . . in secret, the person in charge [being] Harris Isbell, M.D."

Two months later when I had received no reply, I noted in a follow-up letter to the same organizations that "information on the CIA Operation

MKULTRA must be provided as required under the U.S. Freedom of Information Act."

By September 18, 1986, when nearly a year had passed since my first request and I still had not heard, I wrote again and repeated the pertinent details. Half a month later, on October 3, 1986, the State Department notified me that "the material requested appears to have been originated with other agencies," with instructions to contact the following officials:

1) John W. Wright, Information and Privacy Coordinator, Central Intelligence Agency, Washington, DC 20505;

2) Mr. Russell M. Roberts, Director, FOIA/PD Division, Room 118F, Department of Health and Human Services, HHH Building, Washington, DC 20201.

I followed the instructions and wrote to both.

On October 19, 1986, Lee S. Strickland, Information and Privacy Coordinator at the CIA, wrote in answer to request number one: "Our analysts will review your request, and we will be in touch with you and advise of any problems we have encountered, or whether we can search for documents without any additional information. Your request has been assigned Reference No. F86-1217 for identification purposes."

On October 30, 1986, Anderson Springs, FOA Assistant, Office of Public Affairs, Public Health Service, Department of Health and Human Services, replied to request number two:

"Under current Departmental policy, your letter has been referred to the following agency for response: Mrs. Mildred Lehman, Associate Administrator for Communications and Public Affairs, Alcohol, Drug Abuse, & Mental Health Administration (ADAMHA), Room 12c-15, Parklawn Building, 5600 Fishers Lane, Rockville, MD 20857. (301) 443-3783. You should be hearing from ADAMHA shortly."

On November 5, 1986, Lee Strickland again wrote to say,

. . . As you may be aware, research into such matters, funded in part by the CIA under the project name MKULTRA, was conducted, with few exceptions, in various hospitals and institutions with witting volunteers and selectees, under the auspices and control of highly-trained medical professionals.

During a meticulous review of all locatable CIA records of these research activities, we, with one exceptions [*sic*], did not find names of any of the people who took part in the testing either on a witting or unwitting basis. Specifically, after a diligent search, no reference to your name or any names of individuals at Lexington has been discovered.

Accordingly, if you desire records of the individuals that were involved in an Agency-supported behavior control research project at some institution, you should contact the specific institution since it alone would have additional details.

Lastly, please be advised that, pursuant to Department of Justice opinion, no compensation is due owing and none has been paid to participants in the witting projects. Thank you for your interest in the CIA.

Two months later, on January 7, 1987, Winnifred M. Austermann, Associate Administrator for Communications and Public Affairs, AD-AMHA, Public Health Service, Department of Health and Human Services, also replied to request number two as follows: "I am advised that no records exist today at the Addiction Research Center, or elsewhere in this agency, which include the information you are seeking."

On May 18, 1987, Sara Downes of the Information and Privacy Staff at the Department of State finally answered my *two-year-old* inquiry: "Pursuant to your request, a search for responsive documents was initiated with the Department's Central Foreign Policy Records. This records system is the one most likely to maintain the information you requested. The search of the Central Foreign Policy Records has been completed and has resulted in the retrieval of no documents responsive to your request. This now concludes our processing of your request under the Freedom of Information Act."

My reaction to these various communications? Intense frustration, anger, even outrage at this overdose of governmental buck-passing and bureaucratic bullshit. We had the CIA and the military to thank for introducing the LSD that destroyed my father, then promulgating the psychedelic culture that turned our society upside down. Yet I could not find one person paid by my taxes who would look for or disclose the true facts about an American citizen's involuntary subjection to the mind-destroying agent.

In October of 1988, a year and a half after the last of this string of infuriating responses, I gleaned some welcome news: the CIA had compensated eight of Ewen Cameron's Canadian MKULTRA victims for their suffering. *U.S. News & World Report* carried a story headed "A cold-war horror show's last act" with details of the out-of-court settlement. Although one of the original nine plaintiffs had died, the CIA had paid one hundred thousand dollars (Canadian) to each of the eight surviving victims of secret LSD experiments conducted in Montreal—in all, about seven hundred fifty thousand in U.S. dollars. While the original nine plaintiffs had signed consents for Cameron to treat them, not one ever signed a consent to submit to scientific experiments. The CIA made no apologies for its part in the shameful affair, nor did it admit any wrongdoing. An Agency spokesman, Bill Devine, declared, "We have consistently maintained that the actions were appropriate at the time. The standards were different than today."

Different standards? What a disingenuous statement! Inhumanity is inhumanity, abuse of individual rights is nothing less, and sadism is sadism no matter how prettily the CIA would like to dress it up. Everything Cameron did was in utter disregard of the Nuremberg Code. Yet the fact remained that the relatively insignificant settlement was paid. In one sense, at least, these innocent sufferers had won. The *U.S. News* story mentioned a Washington lawyer named James Turner, who investigated the case and represented the plaintiffs. I filed that name away in memory.

Shortly afterward I learned, from an *Atlanta Journal-Constitution* piece by Jacqueline Cutler, of a man a little younger than myself who had gone through suffering remarkably similar to my own—psychiatrist Harvey Weinstein, M.D. Doctor Weinstein's elderly father Lou, a successful self-made Canadian businessman who in middle age had begun to suffer panic attacks, was one of the eight included in the CIA settlement. Doctor Weinstein, who had also undertaken to learn exactly what was done to his father, discovered that after Mr. Weinstein was hospitalized at Allan Memorial for his panic attacks, Cameron destroyed his mind and useful life.

When I obtained a copy of Dr. Weinstein's book about his family's ordeal, I was staggered by the parallel nightmares he and I had lived through. The elder Weinstein's sufferings were even greater than my father's, for he had endured several stays at Allan Memorial, subjected repeatedly to Cameron's "treatments." Unable to attend to business at his dress factory because of the mental incapacity Cameron's abuse had caused, Mr. Weinstein was victimized by a bookkeeper who embezzled thousands of dollars, and lost his livelihood altogether when forced to sell out. Auctioned off piecemeal, the factory brought less than half of what it had once been worth.

The Weinstein family had to sell their substantial home and move to a small apartment, and Mr. Weinstein's ability to function as a normal human being was gone for good.

Young Weinstein took on the role of man of the house during his father's illness and his own formative years, reminding me of the young Georgia boy I once had been. He too dreamed of escaping but was too honorable to abandon his parents to their misery. His older sisters married and left home. His grades fell as mine did. He managed by sheer perseverance and ability to finish medical school and progress to psychiatric training, yet he "put on blinkers," as he described it, "not ready to deal with" any mention of Cameron or his father's ordeal.

Only after he submitted to psychotherapy was he able to function reasonably well in his chosen field. For decades I couldn't talk about what had happened to Daddy or the rest of us. It was only after I began to talk about the grim details with my collaborator on this book that I got any relief from my pain. Like me, Dr. Weinstein remembered his father as an energetic, jovial, fun-loving extrovert, star actor in the drama of a family moving up in the world, whose true personality was destroyed within months after falling into an evil doctor's hands.

THE TORTURES Weinstein's father suffered robbed him utterly of the power to manage his life—an even more drastic outcome than what happened to my dad. Mr. Weinstein became irrational, suffered hallucinations, and was sent home by Cameron on placebos, leaving his family to deal with his irrationality and terrors. In Daddy's case there were no placebos, only self-administered beer.

After Marks's book appeared and Dr. Weinstein read a newspaper piece describing MKULTRA, he experienced his own epiphany precisely as I had done. It was as if, 1,500 miles apart, he and I were acting identical roles in the same play. As he began to look more deeply into Cameron's ghastly actions, the young psychiatrist urged his father to file a lawsuit for damages, but his parents' negative reaction discouraged any solo pursuit of justice. A Washington lawyer asked Dr. Weinstein to try to persuade his father to join other patients in legal action against the CIA; again, the elder Weinsteins dissuaded their son. Not until a year after Dr. Weinstein's mother passed away was he finally able to convince his father to become a party to the suit.

First a seven hundred fifty thousand dollar award to the Olsons, now the same amount to these eight: was seven hundred fifty thousand dollars the CIA's fire-sale price for wrecking human lives?

THE CANADIAN VICTIMS' ordeal, legal struggle, and vindication gave me the courage to push my own crusade further. I decided to go to Washington to meet with their attorney, James Turner. When I read his quote that the experiments "wrecked patients' lives, causing organic brain syndromes and a plethora of lifelong problems such as a loss of memory and concentration," I knew that Turner understood how profound MKULTRA's consequences were. And I could add another affliction to his list—the paranoia we had lived through within my dad.

Jim Turner impressed me favorably and was interested to hear what I had to say, but when I tried to tell my story the words stuck in my mouth. For years I had suffered from a condition called reactive hyperemia—a sudden rush of blood to my face caused by any highly charged emotion. There in Turner's office my face burned, my throat seemed to close, and

I started to cry. I had kept the nightmare locked inside me for so long that I couldn't confess the horrendous psychic cost I had paid. I tried to start over and broke down a second time. Several times more I made the effort, sabotaged by my emotions at every turn. I finally just sat there in Jim Turner's office and wept.

He did his best to reassure and encourage me, but when we both saw that for the moment any attempt to tell the story would be in vain, he said, "Well, Dr. Wall, come back to see me if and when you decide to do something. I'll help you however I can."

I flew back to Atlanta. What would it take to enable me to talk about it, to set the wheels of justice turning? Perhaps Mother would help me. I went to see her in Americus and told her about my discoveries and the trip to Washington.

"Just as soon as I can," I said, "I'm going forward with a lawsuit against Isbell, the CIA, anybody who had anything at all to do with what happened to Daddy."

"My God, son, don't do that! Please. Don't open up that wound again! Living through it once was too much. If you bring it all up again it will kill me."

"Mother, other people have brought court cases and won. Don't you think Daddy deserves as much? Don't you want to see his good name restored?"

"It's over, son. He's dead and gone, the past is the past. I'm old, please don't do this to me. If you care a thing about me, let me live what years I have left in peace."

Her voice and her face betrayed such pain that I knew while she was in this world I could not carry through with my intention. Never mind, one day it would happen.

Over the years my resolve to tell the story grew. I began to mention it to a few close friends, and when one fellow with a published book told me about a book-editing company that might help. I adopted his suggestion, through the company found my collaborator, and together we set out to complete the work. Steady months of interviews, correspondence, research, writing, and revision followed.

Fifty years had passed since the CIA decreed my father's tragic fate, twenty-five since I first discovered its cause. Why now, at this point in my life, was I determined to drag it all up again? Did anyone care?

First and foremost, I cared. My father, a good and decent man, was done a cruel injustice and had his honorable name blackened by men unworthy to wipe his shoes. I intended to clear that name, to see the respect he had so rightfully earned restored.

But I had another, further-reaching reason for wanting the story told. The philosopher George Santayana said it, I believe: "Those who cannot remember the past are condemned to repeat it."

How many Americans are too young to remember the Cold War, with its frantic fears that the Communists might overpower us to rule the world? How many are too young to recall the bomb shelters created in basements and backyards against the terror of nuclear immolation? How many, like my disenchanted ex-wife and many of my friends, cannot believe that a government agency would give a private citizen a drug that would make him crazy, without his consent? Any who refuse to believe in the reality of these horrors may live to see them repeated, or even watch helplessly as those they love become hapless victims of an untrammeled government.

I went to visit Mother as the book began to take shape, I could tell she was failing. The hard times remained painfully vivid in her mind, but she wouldn't talk about them. All the same, I told her I was writing the book. "Let's don't talk about that," she said, and changed the subject. Nevertheless, we forged quietly ahead with our project, and when Mother passed away peacefully just eight months short of her hundredth birthday, I knew it was time to finish Daddy's story.

Now that it's done, I feel satisfied to have carried it through. The story had to be told, and told in full. But the book is only the first part, for the saga's final chapter is still to come—I intend to pursue legal action to justify my father's and my family's suffering. Now that we know why it happened and who was to blame, he would want me to do it, and I can't rest until I do.

The daughter-in-law Jane, and Dr. J. G. Standifer, all of whom are now ghosts, what became of the other agents of Daddy's destruction?

Before his retirement in 1973, MKULTRA mastermind Sidney Gottlieb received one of the CIA's highest honors—the Distinguished Intelligence Medal. Afterward, he destroyed what he thought was the totality of MKULTRA records and walked away from his career to set out with his wife to roam the world. They were traveling by bus in Turkey in 1975 when word reached them of the upcoming Church Committee hearings. Called back to the States to testify, Gottlieb agreed to do so only after assurance of immunity from prosecution. In spite of his lengthy and strenuous recent travels, he pleaded a weak heart and was the only CIA witness permitted to testify from a private room. I suspect he hid out for fear that some enraged victim or victim's family member might come there to kill him.

Ever the liar, unwilling to face up, when asked why he had destroyed the MKULTRA files, he laid it to "a burgeoning paper problem." Questioned about specifics of the MKULTRA program, he either answered vaguely or stated he "couldn't remember." He died in 1999.

In their newsletter *Counterpunch,* the radical journalist Alexander Cockburn and environmental activist Jeffrey St. Clair headlined Gottlieb's passing "U.S. Official Poisoner Dies" and went on to describe him as a "pusher, assassin, and pimp." Harsh words? If the shoe fits . . .

Allen Dulles, the wily old spymaster and CIA director who first gave his stamp of approval to the MKULTRA program, died in 1969.

Richard Helms, defender and primary sponsor of MKULTRA, accepted the National Security Medal from President Reagan before he died and was buried at Arlington National Cemetery in 2002.

Harris Isbell continued to publish in his field and bask in professional acclaim but refused all interviews. He moved around some before dying in 1995, having lived twenty-one years longer than my dad.

While I call myself a Christian, I fervently hope that in the afterlife the Great Master who judgeth all requires an exacting account from every one of those men. Their arrogance and disdain for the lives of thousands of innocent people can scarcely be conceived. The LSD they were responsible for introducing into and disseminating through large sections of our population destroyed countless lives and changed our society forever, in ways few of us can applaud. Both they and their masters had much to answer for.

We live in a perilous age, amid threats great enough to tempt us, as Hoover suggested in 1947, to set aside the old rules of fair play. But we must hold to the high moral ground, tempering our fervor to use any and all weapons at our disposal. America was founded on human rights, and the rights of American citizens are paramount.

As the adage has it, power corrupts, and absolute power corrupts absolutely. We must see that absolute power is never placed in the hands of a reckless, devious, secretive few. "The truth shall make you free," declare both the Gospel of John and the inscription at CIA headquarters—two-thousand-year-old words with vital relevance for our time.

Afterword

What lesson can the MKULTRA horrors teach? What possible connection can my father's downfall, my family's pain have to today's concerns about our intelligence capabilities? Could the World Trade Center terrorists attack disaster of 9/11/01 have been prevented if Congress had not emasculated the CIA after the scandal of illegal drug experiments was exposed? The answer is we don't know, but in a free democratic country like the United States of America there has to be responsible control and monitoring of all governmental agencies by our elected officials.

During the Cold War and MKULTRA's heyday, America's intelligence agencies were flying off in all directions: monopolizing the world supply of LSD and paying scientists to dose untold thousands, many of whom were never told what they got or why; creating poisons to disable or kill and occasionally eliminating a human subject in the process; making every imaginable effort to manipulate the human mind with results that sometimes led to more destroyed lives or even unplanned deaths.

More bizarrely, the CIA plotters sought chemicals to make Fidel Castro's beard fall out, poison Patrice Lumumba's toothpaste, and transmit deadly disease in a poisoned handkerchief to an Iraqi military leader too cozy with the Soviets. And while all these shenanigans were underway, my unsuspecting father was being dosed and driven mad by one of their mind-bending potions.

What was lacking at that time? Accountability, respect for individual human rights as laid out by the Geneva Convention, the Nuremberg Code of medical ethics, and the U.S. Constitution—and finally, plain old common sense.

Today we are paying the price for these misguided schemes and the mendacious and cynical bureaucracy that endorsed them. The 1970s

CIA revelations led to a public outcry, congressional and presidential clampdowns on intelligence activities, and a general housecleaning that severely weakened the agency. In the aftermath, among the capable but disillusioned employees who were not let go, many took early retirement or found other escape routes, while the intelligence bureaucracy piled on more layers that further diffused its powers.

Subsequently officials at all the intelligence agencies, rather than enlarging interagency networking to improve exchange of vital information, kept their distance from the dishonored agency for fear of being tarred with the same brush and losing funding for their own activities. What is the result for our intelligence capabilities today? Too few agents on the ground in trouble spots, too few linguists, too few analysts who understand or are able to work undercover among our country's sworn enemies, twentieth century communications in a twenty-first century world, and territorial antagonisms and competition for funds that make essential change virtually impossible.

Dr. Henry Wall was one pawn among many thousands on the chessboard of what passed for vital intelligence work, until the game became so chaotic as to defeat any attempt to play. We must hope that our public servants now understand how crucial are the rebuilding and fortification of our intelligence systems. Time is of the essence—it is no overstatement to say that our country's fate depends upon their success.

In my father's tragedy I find one inescapable lesson: never again must any American citizen's rights be so callously violated. Never again must any unwilling American become the government's guinea pig, and never again must any intelligence-gathering purpose supersede the protection our Constitution provides.

Acknowledgments

This book could never have been completed without the help of many for whose support, encouragement, and contributions I am most grateful. A special thanks is due to Betsy Tice White of The Editorial Department, LLC, for her outstanding work that made this book possible.

Deep appreciation is due especially to my sister, Anne Wall Williams, for her outstanding courage and never-give-up attitude throughout the family's tragedy and its enduring aftermath. Her enthusiastic support of our undertaking and detailed recall of many painful events made it far easier to get the full story told than it might have been in the absence of her wholehearted help. Thank you, Anne.

A concise biographical article about William Henry Wall, M.D., by my mother, Hallie Walker Wall, appeared in a volume published by the Early County Historical Society, and her faithful preservation of newspaper articles and other memorabilia covering more than fifty years proved invaluable to our task.

My childhood friend Charles Barton Rice, Sr., of Atlanta generously agreed to be interviewed and quoted.

In Early County, we had assistance from many more interviewees, including Juanita and Ernest Turner, Robert Hall, the late William Hudspeth and John Puckett, who lent us the Early County Historical Society volume, and others who preferred to remain anonymous.

In Americus, we found McCall Calhoun, M.D., a delightful conversationalist with a vivid recall of fifty-year-old events and an unstinting respect for the memory of his friend and colleague, Dr. Wall.

Staff at the U. S. Records Depository in East Point, Georgia, were most helpful, as was Dale Couch of the office of the Georgia Secretary of State.

The invaluable expertise and assistance of Trudy Kelly at Mercer University's School of Pharmacy led us to documentation of the time and manner by which Wyeth introduced its product Demerol (meperidine), as well as to the subsequent magazine articles that misled thousands into becoming the narcotic's slaves.

Professor James Cook, Ph.D., of Cedartown, Georgia, was most generous with his time and knowledge. His detailed understanding of twentieth-century government in Georgia enabled us to extract the essence of the complex political stew of the times and present it in a comprehensible way.

Renni Browne line-edited the manuscript with her usual masterful skill. Ross Browne of The Editorial Department served as a tireless cheerleader. Randall Williams at NewSouth Books understood our aim and helped us see the project through.

Finally, Betsy's husband, David, willingly gave up his usual turn at the computer, offered medical knowledge when asked, and served as chauffeur to obtain the necessary interviews.

We thank you, one and all.

Bibliography

"A cold-war horror show's last act," *U.S. News & World Report,* October 17, 1988.

Andrews, H. L. "The development of tolerance to demerol." *Journal of Pharmacology and Experimental Therapeutics,* vol. 76, 1942.

Batterman, Robert C. "Demerol, a New Synthetic Drug—Effectiveness in Man of." Pharmaceutical Abstracts, *Pharmacology, Toxicology and Therapeutics,* 1942.

Cook, James F. *The Governors of Georgia, 1754–1995.* Mercer University Press.

Cutler, Jacqueline. "Doctor Unearthed CIA Plot that Wrecked His Father's Life," *Atlanta Journal & Constitution,* October 16, 1988.

De Kruif, Paul, "God's Own Medicine," *Reader's Digest,* June, 1946.

"Drug Without Addicts," *Newsweek,* September 13, 1943.

Forsyth, Frederick. *Avenger.* Thomas Dunne Books, an imprint of St. Martin's Press, 2003.

"God's Own Narcotic," *TIME,* July 29, 1946.

Gup, Ted, "The Coldest Warrior," *Washington Post,"* December 26, 2001.

Himmelsbach, C. K. "Demerol (1-Methyl-4-Phenyl-Piperidine-4-Carbonic Acid Ethyl Ester) — Addiction Liability of." Pharmaceutical Abstracts, *Pharmacology, Toxicology and Therapeutics,* 1942.

Isbell, Harris. "The search for a nonaddicting analgesic: Has it been worth it?" *Clinical Pharmacology and Therapeutics,* vol. 22, no. 4, October, 1977.

Laurence, William L. "Demerol is Reported Not to be Habit-Forming—Scientists at Boston Told of Discoveries." *The New York Times,* April 2, 1942.

Lee, Martin A., and Bruce Shlain. *Acid Dreams: The Complete Social History of LSD: THE CIA, the Sixties, and Beyond.* Grove Press, 1985.

Marks, John. *The Search for the "Manchurian Candidate": The CIA and Mind Control.* Times Books, 1979.

"Mind-Bending Disclosures: The agency's search for the secret of brainwashing," *TIME,* August 15, 1977.

"New Pain-Killer Is Found," *The New York Times,* April 2, 1942.

Norfleet, Barbara. *When We Liked Ike: Looking for Postwar America.* W. W. Norton & Co., 2001.

Smith, Ken. *Raw Deal.* Blast Books, 1998.

Thomas, Gordon. *Journey Into Madness: The True Story of Secret CIA Mind Control and Medical Abuse.* Bantam Books, 1989.

Wall, Hallie Walker. "William Henry Wall, M.D." *Collections of the Early County Historical Society,* Mary Grist Whitehead, ed., vol. 2, 1979.

"Warns Against Demerol," *The New York Times,* July 11, 1946.

Weinstein, Harvey. *A Father, a Son, and the CIA.* James Lorimer & Co., Toronto, 1988.

Additional information was gleaned from *The Albany Herald*'s coverage of the 1953 trial of Dr. Wall and the two nurses, various *Early County News* items over a period of many years, and editorials and news items from *The Atlanta Journal* and *The Atlanta Constitution* over two decades.